Proverbs

Wisdom from Above

THE
PASSION™
TRANSLATION

Translated from the Hebrew, Aramaic, and Greek Texts
Dr. Brian Simmons

5 Fold Media
Visit us at www.5foldmedia.com

ISBN: 978-1-936578-65-8
Library of Congress Control Number: 2013939794

Endorsements

"Reading through this translation of Proverbs makes me feel as though I'm curled up on the sofa with Papa, downloading His wisdom to direct my journey. I believe *The Passion Translation* has captured the heart behind heaven's instruction, and will layer deep foundations of truth in your life, increasing you in favor, authority, and trust!"

A.J. Butel
Author of Overshadowed

"Brian Simmons has done a remarkable job of making the book of Proverbs come alive on an entirely different level! His scholarly and linguistic brilliance is on open display throughout this book, and you will be hooked from the start with the expanded understanding of the very word *proverb*. However, what Brian does best is connect us to the Hebraic paradigm for experiencing this ancient book of wisdom. For me, it was impossible to not be swept up by the author's own joy of discovery of the hidden treasures of this book. I highly recommend this labor of passion—so get ready to enjoy Proverbs as never before."

Johnny Enlow
Author, Social Reformer

"With the mind of a scholar and the heart of a lover, Brian Simmons combines the best of both worlds for us in his devoted translation work. What a marvelous job my friend and seasoned leader is doing for the body of Christ! I applaud the life and ministry of Dr. Brian Simmons!"

Dr. James W Goll
Founder of Encounters Network
Best-selling Author

"Brian and Candice are friends of the Holy Spirit and it is with His guidance that the Bible is being opened to us with greater clarity than ever before through this translation project. I believe that the release of *The Passion Translation* coincides with a global awakening, and this new translation has been given by God to fuel the fire of this awakening. It was through a life-changing encounter with God that Brian was commissioned to do this translation and I believe that an impartation for Holy Spirit encounters is released through his ministry. I pray that God's Word will provoke you to love as never before as you read *The Passion Translation* and that your hearts will be set ablaze with a fresh passion for God."

Katherine Ruonala
Glory City Church, Brisbane, Australia

"Brian Simmons is a brilliant man who has been given revelation and insight into a deeper meaning of the Scriptures. God has breathed a passion in Brian to see the rich words of the Bible presented to us in a new light. Reading this translation will enlighten your heart, mind, and spirit as you are summoned into the essence of the Man, Christ Jesus' undeniable love for you. I highly recommend this new Bible translation to everyone."

Dr. Ché Ahn
Senior Pastor, HRock Church, Pasadena, CA
President, Harvest International Ministry

Translator's Introduction

The Bible is a book of poetry, not simply starched, stiff doctrines, devoid of passion. The Bible, including Proverbs, is full of poetic beauty, and subtle nuances ripe with meaning. The ancient wisdom of God fills its pages! Proverbs is a book of wisdom from above, tucked inside of metaphors, symbols, and poetic imagery. God could properly be described as the Divine Poet and Master Artisan who crafted the cosmos to portray His glory, and has given us His written Word to reveal His wisdom.

The glory we see in the heavens and in the beauty of creation can also be discerned in the written Word. Inspired from eternity, the sixty-six books of our Bible convey the full counsel and wisdom of God. Do you need wisdom? God has a verse for that!

The Bible begins with seventeen books of historical revelation before the section known as the five books of divine poetry: Job, Psalms, Proverbs, Ecclesiastes, and the Song of Songs. These Scriptures show us the reality of knowing God through experience, not just through history or doctrines. These five books are a progressive revelation of our advancement into God's endless glory.

We start with Job which points us to the end of our self-life to discover the "end" or greatest revelation of the Lord, which is His tender love and wisdom. Then we move on to the Psalms which reveal a new life we enter into with God, expressed through praise and prayer. Next is Proverbs where we enroll in the Divine Seminary of Wisdom and Revelation to learn the ways of God. Then comes Ecclesiastes where we're taught to set our heart not on the things of this life, but on those values which endure eternally. And finally, the sweetest lyrics ever composed lead us into divine romance, where we are immersed in Jesus' love for His bride.

The nature of Hebrew poetry is quite different from English poetry. There is a pleasure found in Hebrew poetry that transcends rhyme and meter. The Hebrew verses come in a poetic package, a form of meaning that imparts an understanding that is deeper than mere logic. True revelation unfolds an encounter—an experience of knowing God as He is revealed through the mysterious vocabulary of riddle, proverb, and parable.

For example, the Hebrew word for proverb, *mashal,* has two meanings. The first meaning is obviously, "parable, byword, metaphor, a pithy saying that expresses wisdom."[a] But the second meaning is overlooked by many. The homonym, *mashal,* can also mean, "to rule, to take dominion," or "to reign with power!"[b]

There is a deep well of wisdom to reign in life and to succeed in our destiny found within this divinely anointed compilation of Proverbs. The wisdom that God has designed for us to receive will cause us to excel, to rise up as rulers-to-be in the earth and in the spiritual realm. The kingdom of God is brought into the earth as we implement the heavenly wisdom of Proverbs!

Although the Proverbs can be interpreted in their most literal and practical sense, the wisdom contained herein is not unlocked by a casual surface reading. The spirit of revelation has breathed upon every verse to embed a deeper meaning. Solomon, the wisest human to ever live, has written a book containing some of the deepest revelation in the Bible. When Solomon pens a proverb, there is more than meets the eye.

Who Are The Proverbs Written To?

This compilation of wisdom's words is written to you! Throughout the book we find words like: "Listen, my sons. Listen, my daughters." It is

---

a. *Strong's Exhaustive Concordance,* H4912.
b. *Strong's Exhaustive Concordance,* H4910.

written to us as sons and daughters of the living God. The teaching we receive is not from a distant God who tells us we better live right or else—but the personal words of love and tenderness from our wise Father, the Father of eternity who speaks right into our hearts with healing, radiant words. Receive deeply the words of the kind Father of heaven as though He were speaking directly to you.

What you have before you now is a dynamic translation of the ancient book of Proverbs. These powerful words are anointed to bring you revelation from the throne room—the wisdom you need to guide your steps and direct your life. You're about to read the greatest book of wisdom ever written, penned by the wisest man to ever live. God gave His servant Solomon this wisdom to pass on to us, His servants, who will complete the last day's ministries of Jesus. What you learn from these verses will change your life and launch you into your destiny.

Next in line for publication in *The Passion Translation* will be *Eternal Love*, the writings of the Apostle John. We are so thankful to all of you who have prayed and supported us in this monumental undertaking of translating the sixty-six books of the inspired Word of God. We especially wish to thank our publishers, Andy and Cathy Sanders at 5 Fold Media and their editorial team for guarding and guiding us along. Their skill and love is deeply appreciated.

So, get ready to be filled to overflowing with the spirit of wisdom and the revelation that God is pouring out in this hour. Proverbs is written for the sons and daughters who have been chosen to rule and reign on the earth. Hang on to every word, for all that God says will bring life to you, a life full of His wisdom from above.

Brian Simmons
brian@passiontranslation.com

This translation is dedicated
To the many wise teachers
Who have helped to shape my life.
I'm especially thankful for the godly leaders
Whose example pointed me
To the ways of Christ.
The astonishing patience they demonstrated
And their life-giving words
Will never be forgotten.

Chapter 1

The Prologue

¹Here are kingdom revelations, words to live by,
And words of wisdom given
To empower you to reign in life,ᵃ
Written as proverbs by
Israel's King Solomon,ᵇ David's son.

²Within these sayings will be found
The revelation of wisdomᶜ
And the impartation of spiritual understanding.
Use them as keys to unlock
The treasures of true knowledge.
³Those who cling to these words
Will receive discipline to demonstrate
Wisdom in every relationship,ᵈ
And to choose what is right and just and fair.
⁴These proverbs will give you great skill
To teach the immature and make them wise,
To give the youth the understanding
Of their design and destiny.

---

a. 1:1 As stated in the introduction, the word for proverbs means more than just a wise saying. It can also mean, "To rule, to reign in power, to take dominion."

b. 1:1 The name *Solomon* means, "Peaceable." There is a greater One than Solomon who gives peace to all His followers; His name is Jesus. Solomon was the seed of David; we are the seed of Jesus Christ. Solomon had an encounter with God after asking for a discerning heart (1 Kings 3:5-14). This pleased God so He gave Solomon wisdom, success, and power. God is ready to impart these same things today for those who ask Him (James 1:5-8).

c. 1:2 There are six Hebrew words for wisdom in the book of Proverbs. Some of these words will require an entire equivalent phrase in English to convey their meaning. The word used here is *chokmah,* and it is used in Proverbs forty-two times. Forty-two is the number of months that Jesus ministered and the number of generations from Abraham to Christ listed in Matthew 1.

d. 1:3 The Hebrew word here is "righteousness." For the Hebrews, righteousness was more than keeping moral laws; it included being righteous in our relationships with others.

Proverbs 1

⁵For the wise, these proverbs
Will make you even wiser,
And for those with discernment,
You will be able to acquire
Brilliant strategies for leadership.
⁶These kingdom revelations
Will break open your understanding
To unveil the deeper meaning of parables,
Poetic riddles and epigrams,
And to unravel the words and enigmas of the wise.

⁷How then does a man gain
The essence of wisdom?
We cross the threshold of true knowledge
When we live in complete awe and adoration of God!ᵃ
Stubborn know-it-allsᵇ
Will never stop to do this,
For they scorn true wisdom and knowledge.

The Wisdom of a Father

⁸Pay close attention, my child,
To your father's wise words
And never forget your mother's instructions.ᶜ
⁹For their insight will bring you success,
Adorning you with grace-filled thoughts,
And giving you reins to guide your decisions.ᵈ

---

a. 1:7 Many translations render this, "the fear of the Lord." This is much more than the English concept of fear; it also implies submission, awe, worship, and reverence. The Hebrew word used here is found fourteen times in Proverbs. The number fourteen (seven times two) represents, "spiritual perfection." The number fourteen is the number mentioned three times in the genealogy of Jesus (Matthew 1:1-7). And it is also the number for "Passover." You will pass from darkness to wisdom's light by the *fear* of the Lord.

b. 1:7 Or, "foolish ones." There are three Hebrew words used for "fool" in Proverbs and another six words that are related to a fool or foolish acts. A fool is described in Proverbs as one who hates true wisdom and correction, with no desire to acquire revelation-knowledge.

c. 1:8 Many expositors see this as the words of David to Solomon, yet we all must give heed to this. The words of our father (God) and our mother, (the church, the freewoman) will bring us wisdom. See Galatians 4:21-31.

d. 1:9 The Hebrew is literally, "adornment for your head, chains for your neck." Our head is a metaphor for our thoughts; our neck, a symbol for willing obedience that guides our decisions, in contrast to being stiff-necked or proud. See Philippians 2:5.

[10]When peer pressure compels you
To go with the crowd,
And sinners invite you to join in,
You must simply say no!
[11]When the gang says,
"We're going to steal and kill,
And still get away with it!
[12]We'll take down the rich and rob them,
We'll swallow them up alive[a]
And take what we want
From whomever we want—
[13]Then we'll take their treasures
And fill our homes with loot!
[14]So come on and join us!
Take your chance with us!
We'll divide up all we get—
We'll each end up with big bags of cash!"
[15]My son, refuse to go with them
And stay far away from them.
[16]For crime is their way of life
And bloodshed their specialty.
[17]To be aware of their snare
Is the best way of escape.
[18]They'll resort to murder
To steal their victim's assets
But eventually it will be their own lives
That are ambushed!
[19]In their ungodly disrespect for God,
They bring destruction on their own lives!

Wisdom's Warning

[20]Wisdom's praises are sung in the streets
And celebrated far and wide.
[21]Wisdom's song is not always heard

---

a. 1:12 Literally, "We'll swallow them alive just like Sheol swallows them whole (i.e. while they still have their riches) and takes them down to the pit." This is a parable of robbing the rich.

Proverbs 1

In the halls of higher learning,
But in the hustle and bustle of everyday life,
Its lyrics can be heard
Above the din of the crowd.[a]
You'll hear wisdom's warning
As she preaches courageously
To those who stop to listen:
[22]"Foolish ones, how much longer
Will you cling to your deception?[b]
How much longer will you mock wisdom—
Cynical scorners who fight the facts?
[23]Come back to your senses
And be restored to reality—
Don't even think about refusing My rebuke!
Don't you know that I'm ready to pour out
My Spirit of wisdom upon you
And bring to you the revelation of My words
That will make your heart wise?
[24]I've called to you over and over—
Still you refuse to come to Me!
I've pleaded with you again and again,
Yet you've turned a deaf ear to My voice!
[25]Because you have laughed at My counsel
And have insisted on continuing
In your stubbornness,
[26]I will laugh when your calamity comes
And will turn away from you
At the time of your disaster.
Make a joke of My advice, will you?
Then I'll make a joke out of you!
[27]When the storm clouds of terror
Gather over your head,
When dread and distress consume you,

---

a. 1:21 Literally translated, this verse reads, "Wisdom sings out in the streets, and speaks her voice in the squares, crying out at the head of noisy crowds, and at the entrance of the city gates." This is a parabolic statement of wisdom being heard everywhere and in every place.
b. 1:22 Or, "Childish ones, how long will you love your childishness?"

And your catastrophe comes like a hurricane,
[28]Then you will cry out to Me but I won't answer—
Then it'll be too late to expect My help!
When desperation drives you to search for Me
I'll be nowhere to be found—
[29]Because you have turned up your nose at Me
And closed your eyes to the facts,
And have refused to worship Me in awe.[a]
[30]Because you scoffed at My wise counsel
And laughed at My correction—
[31]Now you'll eat the bitter fruit of your own ways!
You've made your own bed, now lie in it!
So how do you like that?
[32]Like an idiot you've turned away from Me
And chosen destruction instead;
Your self-satisfied smugness[b] will kill you!
[33]But the one who always listens to Me
Will live undisturbed in a heavenly peace.
Free from fear;
Confident and courageous you'll rest
Unafraid and sheltered
From the storms of life."

Chapter 2

Searching for Wisdom

[1]My child, only when you treasure My wisdom,
Will you acquire it.
And only if you accept My advice
And hide it within,

---

a. 1:29 The Hebrew-Aramaic word used here can be translated, "fear, dread, awe, and worship." Most translations ignore the other aspects of the Aramaic word *dekhlatha* and the Hebrew word *yirah*. The New Testament tells us there is no fear of condemnation in His love. See 1 John 4:18.
b. 1:32 Or, "your abundant prosperity."

Proverbs 2

Will you succeed.
²So train your heart to listen when I speak
And open your spirit wide
To expand your discernment—
Then pass it on to your sons.[a]
³Yes, cry out for comprehension
And intercede for insight,
⁴For if you keep seeking it
Like a man would seek for sterling silver,
Searching in hidden places
For cherished treasure,
⁵Then you will discover the fear of God
And truly worship Him in the awe and wonder
That He deserves!

⁶Wisdom is a gift from a generous God
And every word He speaks is full of revelation,
And becomes a living fountain of
Understanding within you.[b]
⁷⁻⁸For the Lord has a
Hidden storehouse of wisdom
Made accessible to His godly lovers.[c]
He becomes your personal bodyguard
As you follow His ways;
Protecting and guarding you
As you choose what is right.
⁹Then you will discover all that is just and fair,
And empower you to make the right decisions
As you walk into your destiny.

¹⁰When wisdom wins your heart
And revelation breaks in,
True pleasure enters your soul.
¹¹If you choose to follow good counsel,
Divine design will watch over you and

---

a. 2:2 As translated from the Septuagint.
b. 2:6 The Septuagint adds, "found in His presence."
c. 2:7-8 Or, "the righteous."

Understanding will protect you
From making poor choices.
[12]It will rescue you from evil in disguise
And from those who speak duplicities,
[13]For they have left the highway of holiness
And walk in the ways of darkness.
[14]They take pleasure when evil prospers
And thoroughly enjoy a lifestyle of sin,
[15]But they're walking on a path to nowhere,
Wandering away into deeper deception.

Wisdom, the Way of the Pure

[16]For only wisdom can save you
From the flattery of
The promiscuous woman—
She's such a smooth talking seductress!
[17]She left her husband
And has forgotten her wedding vows.[a]
[18]You'll find her house on the road to hell,
[19]And all the men who go through her doors
Will never come back to the place they were—
They'll find nothing but desolation and despair.

[20]Follow those who follow wisdom
And stay on the right path.
[21]For all My godly lovers
Will enjoy life to the fullest
And will inherit their destinies.[b]

---

a. 2:17 Clearly, this is a warning to those who would commit adultery, but there is a deeper meaning within this text. Proverbs tells us of two women—the adulteress and the virtuous woman of Proverbs 31. Both women speak a parable of two systems in the church. One is religious and alluring, tempting the young anointed ones to come to her "bed" of compromise (Mark 7:13). Her house is not what you may think. The other is the holy bride, virtuous and pure, keeping her first love (her "wedding vows") for Christ alone. Her "house" is the house of the Lord. One system brings shame and despair; the other brings favor, honor, and glory. It is wisdom that protects us from the one, and unites us to the other. See Jeremiah 50-52 and Revelation 17-18.
b. 2:21 Literally, "shall dwell in the land."

²²But the treacherous ones who love darkness
Will not only lose all they could have had—
They'll lose even their own souls! 1/25/ 14 10:15/ PM

Chapter 3

The Rewards of Wisdom

¹⁻²My child, if you truly want a long and satisfying life,
Never forget the things that I've taught you.
Follow closely every truth that I've given you
Then you will have a full and rewarding life.
³Hold on to loyal love and don't let go,
And be faithful to all that you've been taught.
Let your life be shaped by integrity[a]
With truth written upon your heart.
⁴That's how you will find favor and understanding
With both God and men—
You'll gain the reputation of living life well.

Wisdom's Guidance

⁵Trust in the Lord completely,
And not your own opinions,
But with all your heart rely on Him to guide you,
And He will lead you in all the decisions you make.
⁶Become intimate with Him
In whatever you do,
And He'll lead you wherever you go.[b]
And don't think for a moment that you know it all,[c]
⁷For wisdom comes when you adore Him
With awe and wonder,
And avoid everything that's wrong—
⁸For then you'll find the healing refreshment

---

a. 3:3 Or, "tie them around your neck." The neck is a symbol of our will and conscience.
b. 3:6 Or, "He will cut a straight path before you."
c. 3:6 We should always be willing to listen to correction and instruction.

Your body and spirit longs for.[a]
[9]Glorify God with all your wealth,
Honoring Him with your very best[b],
With every increase that comes to you.
[10]And then every dimension of your life
Will overflow with blessings
From an uncontainable source of inner joy!

Wisdom's Correction

[11]My child, when the Lord God speaks to you,
Never take His Words lightly,
And never be upset when He corrects you.
[12]For the Father's discipline comes only
From His passionate love and pleasure for you.
And even when it seems like His correction is harsh,
It's still better than any father on earth gives to his child.
[13]Those who find true wisdom
Obtain the tools for understanding—
The proper way to live,[c]
For they will have a fountain of blessing
Pouring into their lives.
To gain the riches of wisdom is far greater
Than gaining the wealth of the world.
[14]As wisdom increases a great treasure is imparted,
Greater than many bars of refined gold.
[15]It's a more valuable commodity
Than gold and gemstones[d]
For there is nothing you desire
That could compare to her!
[16]Wisdom extends to you long life in one hand

---

a. 3:8 Literally, "healing to your navel and moistening to your bones." The blood supply for a baby in the womb comes through the navel. New cells are made in the marrow of our bones. As the navel and bones picture the life-flow of our bodies, so the navel and bones are also a picture of our inner being. See John 7:37-39.
b. 3:9 Or, "the firstfruits."
c. 3:13 The Hebrew-Aramaic text implies that wisdom gives the ability to take raw facts and draw right conclusions and meaning from them.
d. 3:15 The Hebrew word can also refer to rubies, corals, or pearls.

Proverbs 3

With wealth and promotion[a] in the other.
Out of her mouth flows righteousness
And her words release both law and mercy.[b]
[17]The ways of wisdom are sweet,
Always drawing you
Into the place of wholeness.[c]
[18]Seeking for her brings
The discovery of untold blessings,
For she is the healing Tree of Life
To those who taste her fruits.[d]

Wisdom's Blueprints

[19]The Lord laid earth's foundations
With Wisdom's blueprints,
And by His living-understanding
All the universe came into being.[e]
[20]By His divine revelation
He broke open the hidden fountains of the deep,
Bringing secret springs to the surface
As the mist of the night dripped down from heaven.[f]

Wisdom, Our Hiding Place

[21]My child, set these two goals for your life:
To walk in wisdom,
And to discover discernment[g]—
Don't ever forget how they empower you.
[22]For they strengthen you inside and out

a. 3:16 Or "honor."
b. 3:16 The Greek Septuagint adds this last sentence that is not found in the Hebrew.
c. 3:17 The Hebrew word used here can also mean "peace," or "prosperity."
d. 3:18 Verses 17 and 18 are recited in contemporary Torah services as the Torah scroll is returned to the ark where it is kept.
e. 3:19 When compared with Colossians 1:16, we can see from this verse that Wisdom is a title used in Proverbs for the living Wisdom, Jesus Christ. See also 1 Corinthians 1:30.
f. 3:20 The dew is a metaphor of the Holy Spirit, who comes from the heavens and drenches us with God's presence. See Genesis 27:28; Deuteronomy 32:2; Judges 6:37-40; and Psalm 133:3.
g. 3:21 Like many Hebrew words, there are various possible translations. The word *discernment* can also mean, "discretion, counsel, meditation, and purpose."

And inspire you to do what's right;[a]
You'll be energized and refreshed
By the healing they bring.
[23]They give you living hope to guide you,
And not one of life's tests will cause you to stumble.
[24]You will sleep like a baby, safe and sound—
Your rest will be sweet and secure!
[25]You'll not be subject to terror
For it will not terrify you,
Nor will the disrespectful be able to push you aside[b]
[26]Because God is your confidence in times of crisis,
Keeping your heart at rest in every situation.[c]

Wisdom in Relationships

[27]Why would you withhold payment on your debt
When you have the ability to pay? Just do it![d]
[28]When your friend comes to ask you for a favor,
Why would you say, "Perhaps tomorrow,"
When you have the money right there
In your pocket? Help them today!
[29]Why would you hold a grudge[e] in your heart
Toward your neighbor who lives right next door?
[30]And why would you quarrel with another
When they've done nothing wrong to you?
Is that a chip on your shoulder?[f]
[31]Don't act like those bullies
Or learn their ways.
[32]Every violent thug is despised by the Lord,
But every tender lover finds friendship with God
And will hear His intimate secrets.[g]
[33]The wicked walk under God's constant curse

---

a. 3:22 Or, "adorn your neck." The neck is a picture of our will and conscience.
b. 3:25 As translated from the Septuagint.
c. 3:26 Or, "keeping your foot from being caught."
d. 3:27 The Hebrew is literally, "Don't withhold *wealth* from its owners." See Romans 13:7.
e. 3:29 Or, "plot evil."
f. 3:30 See Romans 12:18.
g. 3:32 See Psalm 25:14.

But godly lovers walk under a stream of His blessing—
For they seek to do what is right!
[34]If you walk with the mockers you'll learn to mock,
But God's grace and favor flows to the meek.[a]
[35]Stubborn fools fill their lives with disgrace,
But glory and honor rests upon the wise.

Chapter 4

A Father's Instruction

[1]Listen to my correction, my sons,
For I speak to you as your father.[b]
Let discernment enter your heart
And you will grow wise
With the understanding I impart.
[2]My revelation-truth[c] is a gift to you
So remain faithful to my instruction.
[3]For I, too, was once the delight of my father[d]
And cherished by my mother, their beloved child.[e]
[4]Then my father taught me, saying:
"Never forget my words.
If you do everything that I teach you,
You'll reign in life!"[f]
[5]So make wisdom your quest—
Search for the revelation of life's meaning.
Don't let what I say go in one ear and out the other!
[6]Stick with wisdom and she will stick to you,
Protecting you throughout your days.
She'll rescue all those

a. 3:34 See James 4:6 and 1 Peter 5:5.
b. 4:1 Read and study this entire chapter as though it were Jesus Christ speaking to you. He is called the everlasting Father and we are called His sons. See Isaiah 9:6-7 and Revelation 21:6-7.
c. 4:2 Literally, *Torah*.
d. 4:3 See Matthew 17:5 and John 3:35.
e. 4:3 Or "unique." See Luke 1-2.
f. 4:4 The lessons of wisdom are meant to be passed from parents to children.

Who passionately listen to her voice.[a]
[7]Wisdom is the most valuable commodity—
So buy it!
Revelation-knowledge is what you need—
So invest in it!
[8]Wisdom will exalt you
When you exalt her truth![b]
She will lead you to honor and favor
When you live your life by her insights.
[9]You'll be adorned with beauty and grace[c]
And wisdom's glory will wrap itself around you,[d]
Making you victorious in the race.

Two Pathways

[10]My sons, if you will take the time
To stop and listen to me
And embrace what I say,
You'll live a long and happy life,
Full of understanding in every way.
[11]I've taken you by the hand in wisdom's ways,
Pointing you to the path of integrity.
[12]Your progress will have no limits
When you come along with me,
And you will never stumble
As you walk along the way.
[13]So receive my correction
No matter how hard it is to swallow,
For wisdom will snap you back into place;
Her words will be invigorating life to you.
[14]So don't detour into darkness
Or even set foot on that path.

---

a. 4:6 It is not enough to acquire wisdom, we must love her and listen wholeheartedly to her instruction.
b. 4:8 The Septuagint is, "build a fort for wisdom and she will lift you high."
c. 4:9 Literally, "she will place a garland of grace on your head and a crown of beauty upon you." The metaphors of a garland and crown are emblems of what is awarded a victor in a race. See 1 Corinthians 9:24-25.
d. 4:9 Or, "wisdom's laurel of glory shielding you."

[15]Stay away from it;
Don't even go there!
[16]For troublemakers are restless
If they're not involved in evil.
And they're not ever satisfied
Until they've brought someone harm.
[17]They feed on darkness
And drink until they're drunk
On the wine of wickedness.[a]
[18]But the lovers of God walk on the highway of light[b]
As their way shines brighter and brighter
Until they bring forth the perfect day!
[19]But the wicked walk in thick darkness—
Like those who travel in fog
And yet don't have a clue
Why they keep stumbling!

Healing Words

[20]Listen carefully, my dear child,
To everything that I teach you
And pay attention to all that I have to say.
[21]Fill your thoughts with my words
Until they penetrate deep into your spirit.[c]
[22]Then as you unwrap my words[d]
They will impart to you true life
And radiant health
Into the very core of your being.
[23]So above all, guard the affections of your heart
For they affect all that you are.
Out of your innermost being
Flows the wellspring of life.
[24]Avoid dishonest speech and pretentious words.
Be free from using perverse words—no matter what!

---

a. 4:17 Or "violence."
b. 4:18 Or, "the glow of sunlight."
c. 4:21 See Colossians 3:16.
d. 4:22 Or, "discover my words."

Watch Where You're Going

[25]Set your gaze on the path before you
And with fixed purpose, looking straight ahead,
Ignore life's distractions.[a]
[26]Watch where you're going!
Stick to the path of truth,
And the road will be safe and smooth before you.
[27]Don't allow yourself to
Be sidetracked for even a moment,
Or take the detour that leads to darkness.

Chapter 5

Avoid Promiscuity

[1]Listen to me, my son,
For I know what I'm talking about.
Listen carefully to my advice
[2]So that wisdom and discernment
Will enter your heart,
And then the words you speak
Will express what you've learned.
[3]Remember this:
The lips of a seductress seem sweet like honey,
And her smooth words are like music in your ears.[b]
[4]But I promise you this:
In the end all you'll be left with
Is a bitter conscience,[c]
For the sting of your sin
Will pierce your soul like a sword!

a. 4:25 Implied in the text. See also Hebrews 12:1-2.
b. 5:3 Some Jewish expositors view this "promiscuous" woman as a metaphor for heresy. She seduces, deceives, and drags to hell. For the believer, the promiscuous woman can be a picture of the false anointing of the religious spirit that attempts to seduce, weaken our message, and rob the anointing of God from our ministries. Of course, there is also a clear and dire warning to all, to stay sexually pure or face the consequences.
c. 5:4 Or, "bitter as wormwood." See Revelation 8:10-11.

Proverbs 5

⁵She'll ruin your life and drag you down to death,
And lead you straight to hell!ᵃ
⁶She has prevented many from
Considering the paths of life.
Yes, she'll take you with her
Where you don't want to go:
Sliding down a slippery road,
Not even realizing
Where the two of you will end up!
⁷Listen to me, young men,
And don't you forget one thing I'm telling you—
Run away from her as fast as you can!
⁸Don't even go near the door of her house,
Unless you want to fall into her seduction.
⁹In disgrace you'll relinquish your honor to another,
And all your remaining years will be squandered—
Given over to the cruel one.ᵇ
¹⁰Why would you let strangers
Take away your strengthᶜ
While the labors of your house
Go to someone else?
¹¹For as you grow old,
You'll groan in anguish and shameᵈ
As sexually transmitted diseases
Consume your body.ᵉ
¹²And then finally you'll admit
That you were wrong, and say,
"If only I had listened to wisdom's voice
And not stubbornly demanded my own way,
Because my heart hated to be told what to do!
¹³"Why didn't I take seriously
The warning of my wise counselors?

---

a. 5:5 Or "sheol." This is the Aramaic and Hebrew word for the place of the dead. The Greeks call it "hades." Sheol is not eternal but will be destroyed. See Hosea 13:14 and Revelation 20:14.
b. 5:9 This would be the devil who torments the conscience as the result of this sin.
c. 5:10 Or, "wealth." This could also refer to spiritual strength and wealth.
d. 5:11 The Hebrew word for "groan" is also used for the roar of a lion or the ocean's roar.
e. 5:11 Implied in the context of the topic of sexual promiscuity. The Hebrew is, "diseases."

Why was I so stupid to think
That I could get away with it?
[14]"Now I'm totally disgraced
And my life is ruined!
I'm paying the price—
For the people of the congregation
Are now my judges!"[a]

Sex Reserved for Marriage

[15]My son, share your love with your wife alone.
Drink from her well of pleasure and from no other.
[16]Why would you have sex with a stranger,
Or with anyone other than her?
[17]Reserve this pleasure for you and her alone
And not with another.[b]
[18]Your sex life will be blessed[c]
As you take joy and pleasure
In the wife of your youth!
[19]Let her breasts be your satisfaction,[d]
And let her embrace[e]
Intoxicate you at all times—
Be continually delighted and
Ravished with her love!
[20]My son, why would you be exhilarated
By an adulteress—
By embracing a woman[f]
That is not yours?
[21]For God sees everything you do

---

a. 5:14 See John 8:1-11.
b. 5:17 Because of the sudden change in the Hebrew text to the masculine gender ("stranger" or "another"), there is at least an inference that men having sex with men, or with a woman who is not your wife, is forbidden.
c. 5:18 The Hebrew includes the word, "fountain" which is an obvious metaphor for the sex act. Interestingly, the root word for fountain can also refer to the eyes. It may be a poetic subtlety that the eyes should only be on your wife, not on the nakedness of another. See v.19.
d. 5:19 The Hebrew includes a picturesque metaphor of the wife being like a "friendly deer and a favored filly."
e. 5:19 The Septuagint reads, "Let her share conversation with you."
f. 5:20 Or "breasts."

And His eyes are wide open, as He
Observes every single habit you have.
²²Beware that your sins don't overtake you,
And the scars of your own conscience
Become the ropes that tie you up!
²³Those who choose wickedness
Die for lack of self-control,
For their foolish ways lead them astray.
Carrying them away as hostages—
Kidnapped captives robbed of destiny.ᵃ

Chapter 6

Words of Wisdom

¹My son, if you cosign a loan for an acquaintance,
And guarantee their debt,
You'll be sorry that you ever did it!
²You'll be trapped by your promise
And legally bound by the agreement,
So listen carefully to my advice—
³Quickly get out of it if you possibly can!
Swallow your pride, get over your embarrassment,
And go tell your "friend" you want your nameᵇ
Off that contract!
⁴Don't put it off, and don't rest until you get it done!
⁵Rescue yourself from future painᶜ
And be free from it once and for all.
You'll be so relieved that you did!ᵈ

Life Lessons

⁶When you're feeling lazy, come and learn a lesson
From the tale of the tiny ant.

---

a. 5:23 Implied in the context.
b. 6:3 There is an implication in the Hebrew that the one whose loan was cosigned for is no longer a friend. The Hebrew word can also be translated, "apostate."
c. 6:5 Implied in the context.
d. 6:5 The life lesson to learn is that even when considering something that seems to be good, there may be unexpected consequences that should be considered before obligating yourself.

Yes, all you lazybones come learn from
The example of the ant and enter into wisdom.
[7]The ant has no chief, no boss, nor manager—
Yet no one has to tell them what to do.
[8]You'll see them working and toiling all summer long,
Stockpiling their food in preparation for winter.
[9]So wake up, sleepyhead, how long will you lie there?
When will you wake up and get out of bed?
[10]If you keep nodding off and thinking "I'll do it later,"
Or say to yourself, "I'll just sit back awhile and take it easy,"
Excuses, excuses—now watch how the future unfolds!
[11]You'll learn what it means to go without!
Poverty will pounce on you like a bandit[a]
And move in as your roommate for life![b]
[12-13]Here's another life lesson to learn
From observing the wayward and wicked man[c]—
You can tell they're lawless.
They're constant liars, proud deceivers,
Full of clever ploys and convincing plots.[d]
[14]Their twisted thoughts are perverse,
Always with a scheme to stir up trouble,
And sowing strife with every step they take.
[15]But when calamity comes knocking on their door,
Suddenly and without warning they're undone—
Broken to bits, shattered with no hope of healing.[e]

---

a. 6:11 Or, "vagabond." The Hebrew is literally, "one who walks (away)."
b. 6:11 The life lesson from Solomon's parable: The ant only lives six months, yet stores more food than it will consume. So we should learn the wisdom of preparing for the future and learn frugality in the present. Don't put off for the future, the preparations you should make today. Now is always better than later. Today is the day to choose what's right and serve the Lord.
c. 6:12-13 The Hebrew word for "wayward and lawless" here is actually, "a man of Belial." This is a metaphor that is also used elsewhere in the Bible for a worthless man who worships other gods. Additionally, the name *Belial* is found in numerous Dead Sea scrolls as a term for Satan.
d. 6:12-13 The Hebrew gives a picture of one who "winks their eyes, shuffles their feet, and points their finger." This is figure of speech for the devious ways of the wicked.
e. 6:15 The life lesson here is this: The clever and devious may look like they're getting ahead in life, but their path guarantees destruction with no one to help them in it.

27

Proverbs 6

Seven Things God Hates

[16]There are six evils God truly hates
And a seventh[a] that is an abomination to Him:
[17]Putting others down while considering yourself superior—
Spreading lies and rumors—
Spilling the blood of the innocent—
[18]Plotting evil in your heart toward another—
Gloating over doing what's plainly wrong—
[19]Spouting lies in false testimony—
And stirring up strife between friends.[b]
These are entirely despicable to God![c]

[20]My child, obey your father's godly instruction
And follow your mother's life-giving teaching[d];
[21]Fill your heart with their advice and
Let your life be shaped by what they've taught you.[e]
[22]Their wisdom will guide you wherever you go
And keep you from bringing harm to yourself.
Their instruction will whisper to you at every sunrise,
And direct you through a brand new day.
[23]For truth[f] is a bright beam of light—
Shining into every area of your life,
Instructing and correcting you
To discover the ways to godly living.

Truth or Consequences

[24-25]Truth will protect you from immorality,
And from the promiscuity of another man's wife.
Your heart won't be enticed by her flatteries,[g]

---

a. 6:16 The number seven is the number of fullness and completion. The poetic form here is stating that evil in its fullness is an abomination to God.
b. 6:19 The Aramaic is, "deception among brothers."
c. 6:19 A summary statement implied in the context.
d. 6:20 For the New Testament believer, our mother is the church who nurtures us and feeds us life-giving words. See Galatians 4:21-31.
e. 6:21 Or, "bind their words on your heart, and tie them around your neck."
f. 6:23 Or *Torah*.
g. 6:24-25, Or, "don't let her captivate you with her fluttering eyelids."

Or lust over her beauty—
Nor will her suggestive ways conquer you!
[26]Prostitutes reduce a man to poverty,[a]
And the adulteress steals your soul—
She may even cost you your life![b]
[27]For how can a man light his pants on fire
And not be burned?
[28]Can he walk over hot coals of fire[c]
And not blister his feet?
[29]What makes you think that you can sleep
With another man's wife and not get caught?
Do you really think you'll get away with it?
Don't you know it will ruin your life?
[30]You can almost excuse a thief
If he steals to feed his own family.
[31]But if he's caught,
He still has to pay back what he stole sevenfold;
His punishment and fine will cost him greatly.
[32]Don't be so stupid as to think
You can get away with your adultery;
It will destroy your life,[d]
And you'll pay the price for the rest of your days!
[33]You'll discover what humiliation,
Shame, and disgrace are all about,
For no one will ever let you forget what you've done!
[34]A husband's jealousy makes a man furious;
He won't spare you when he comes to take revenge!
[35]Try all you want to talk your way out of it—
Offer him a bribe and see if you can
Manipulate him with your money!
Nothing will turn him aside
When he comes to you
With vengeance in his eyes!

---

a. 6:26 Or, "beg for a loaf of bread."
b. 6:26 The Hebrew is literally, "she hunts for your precious soul."
c. 6:28 A picture of the lusts of the flesh.
d. 6:32 Or, "the destroyer of his soul will do this."

Chapter 7

Wisdom, Your True Love

[1]Stick close to my instruction, my son,
And follow all my advice.
[2]If you do what I say, you'll live well.
Guard your life with my revelation-truth
For my teaching is as precious as your eyesight.[a]
[3]Treasure my instructions,
And cherish them within your heart.[b]
[4]Say to wisdom: "I love you."
And to understanding:
"You're my sweetheart."
[5] "May the two of you protect me,
And may we never be apart!"
For they will keep you from the adulteress
With her smooth words meant to seduce your heart.

[6]Looking out the window of my house one day,
[7]I noticed among the mindless crowd
A simple, naïve young man
Who was about to go astray—
[8]There he was, walking down the street.
Then he turned the corner, going on his way
As he hurried on to the house of the harlot—
The woman he had planned to meet.
[9]There he was in the twilight
As darkness fell;
Thinking no one was watching,
He entered the black shadows of hell.[c]
[10]That's when their rendezvous began
As a woman of the night appeared,
Dressed to kill the strength of any man.
She was decked out as a harlot,

---

a. 7:2 Or, "like you would the pupil of your eye," Literally, "the little man of the eye," which is a figure of speech for your most prized possession.
b. 7:3 Or, "write them upon the tablets of your heart."
c. 7:9 Implied from verse 27.

30

To pursue her amorous plan.
[11]Her voice so seductive, rebellious, and boisterous
As she wanders so far from what's right
Pursuing her amorous plan.
[12]Her "type" can be found
Soliciting on street corners
On just about any night.[a]
[13]So she wrapped her arms around
The senseless young man and
Held him tight— she enticed him
With kisses which seemed so right.
Then, with insolence she whispered in his ear,
[14]"Come with me; it'll be all right.
I've got everything we need for a feast;
I'll cook you a wonderful dinner,[b]
So here I am—I'm all yours!
[15]You're the very one I've looked for;
The one I truly wanted from the moment I saw you.
That's why I've come out here tonight
So that I could meet a man like you![c]
[16]I've spread my canopy bed with coverings,
Lovely multi-colored Egyptian linens

---

a. 7:12 This parable not only warns against the obvious evils of adultery and immorality, but also serves as a warning to anointed young men and women in ministry to not be seduced by the religious system. Wisdom looks from the window (revelation and insight – Ezekiel 8) of her house (the true church of Jesus) and sees a young man (not fully mature—1 John 2:12-14) who placed himself in the path of sin. This made him vulnerable to the seduction of the "harlot," a system of works dependent on religion that entices him into her *bed* (partnership, covering and ordination with her and her system—see Revelation 17-18) "covered with Egyptian linens" (Egypt is a picture of the world system that holds people in bondage). She is "loud and stubborn" (indicative of the old self-life that was never dealt with) and will not remain in her "house" (the true church of Jesus). She lives in the darkness of compromise and her ways are the ways of death. She doesn't remain faithful to her husband (the Bridegroom: God). The two women of Proverbs are the harlot mentioned here and the virtuous woman found in chapter 31, which both speak of two systems of worship. One is true and virtuous; the other is false and seductive.
b. 7:14 Or, "offered peace offerings and paid my vows [in the temple]." This is a way of saying, "I have lots of meat left over from the sacrifices I've offered, enough for a great meal."
c. 7:15 Compared to Song of Songs 3:4, this seems to be a parodic reversal of the Shulamite who goes out into the city to seek a man, finds him, and embraces him. The entire account of the harlot appears to be the converse of the theme of the Song of Songs.

Spread and ready for you to lie down on—
[17]I've sprinkled the sheets with intoxicating perfume;
Made from myrrh, aloes, and sweet cinnamon.[a]
[18]Come, let's get comfortable
And take pleasure in each other
And make love all night!
[19]"There's no one home
For my husband's away on business.
[20]He left home loaded with money to spend,
So don't worry, he won't be back
Until another month ends!"[b]
[21-22]He was swayed by her sophistication,
Enticed by her longing embrace.
She led him down the wayward path
Right into sin and devastation!
So quickly he went astray
With no clue where he was truly headed—
Taken like a dumb ox alongside of the butcher!
Like a venomous snake coiled to strike,
She set her fangs into him![c]
[23]He's like a man about to be executed
With an arrow through his heart,
Like a bird that flies into the net
Unaware what's about to happen!

[24]So listen to me, you young men,
You better take my words seriously!
[25]Control your sexual urges
And guard your heart from lust!

---

a. 7:17 Although these spices are found in the sacred anointing oil, the adulteress (and the system she represents) has only a false anointing with no true power.

b. 7:20 Or, "he left with a bag of money and won't be back until the full moon."

c. 7:21-22 This last sentence is arguably a difficult verse to translate with many variant options. The Aramaic is, "taken like a dog to captivity." The Hebrew can be translated, "bounding like a stag to a trap." Other ancient Jewish commentaries refer to this portion as, "rushing like a venomous snake to discipline the foolish one," meaning, with the swiftness of a snake striking its prey, a fool lunges into his own destruction.

Don't let your passions get out of hand
And don't lock your eyes onto a beautiful woman.
Why would you want to even get close
To temptation and seduction,
To have an affair with her?
[26]She's pierced the souls of multitudes of men—
Many mighty ones have fallen,
And have been brought down by her![a]
[27]If you're looking for the road to hell,
Just go looking for her house!

Chapter 8

Wisdom Calling

[1-3]Can you hear the voice of Wisdom?[b]
From the top of the mountains of influence
She speaks into the gateways
Of the glorious city.[c]
At the place where pathways merge,
At the entrance of every portal,
There she stands,
Ready to impart understanding,
Shouting aloud to all who enter,
Preaching her sermon
To those who will listen.[d]

---

a. 7:26 The Aramaic is even more descriptive, "She has slain a multitude of mighty ones; they've all been killed by her!"

b. 8:1-3 Wisdom is personified throughout the Book of Proverbs. Lady Wisdom is a figure of speech for God Himself who invites us to receive the best way to live, the excellent and noble way of life found in Jesus Christ. Jesus is Wisdom personified, for He was anointed with the spirit of wisdom. See 1 Corinthians 1:30; Colossians 2:3; and Isaiah 11:1-2.

c. 8:1-3 As translated from the Aramaic. The church is also a gateway, the house of God, the portal to heaven, that Jesus calls a "city" set on a hill. Christ is the Head of the church, where the wisdom of God is revealed. See 1 Corinthians 1 and Ephesians 3:10-12.

d. 8:1-3 In chapter 7, it was the harlot calling out to the simple, here it is Lady Wisdom. True wisdom is easy to find; we only have to listen to her voice. Though it comes from above, it is found on the street level. Creation and conscience are two voices that speak to our hearts. To discover wisdom, we don't need a brilliant intellect, but a tender, attentive heart.

Proverbs 8

⁴I'm calling to you, sons of Adam
Yes, and to your daughters as well.[a]
⁵Listen to Me
And you will be prudent and wise.
For even the foolish and feeble
Can receive an understanding heart
That will change their inner being.[b]
⁶The meaning of my words
Will release within you
Revelation for you to reign in life.[c]
My lyrics will empower you
To live by what is right.
⁷For everything I say is unquestionably true,
And I refuse to endure the lies of lawlessness—
My words will never lead you astray.
⁸All the declarations of my mouth can be trusted;
They contain no twisted logic
Or perversion of the truth.
⁹All My words are clear and straightforward
To all who possess spiritual understanding.
If you have an open mind,
You'll receive revelation-knowledge.
¹⁰My wise correction is
More valuable than silver or gold;
The finest gold is nothing compared
To the revelation-knowledge I can impart.
¹¹Wisdom is so priceless
That it exceeds the value of any jewel.[d]
Nothing you could wish for can equal her.
¹²For I am Wisdom, and I am shrewd and intelligent.
I have at My disposal living-understanding
To devise a plan for your life.
¹³Wisdom pours into you when you begin to hate

---

a. 8:4 Implied in the text.
b. 8:5 Implied in the text.
c. 8:6 The Hebrew is literally, "princely" or "noble" things. The implication is that these words of wisdom are for ruling and "reigning in life."
d. 8:11 Literally, "corals" or "pearls."

Every form of evil in your life,
For that's what worship and fearing God is all about.
You will discover that your pompous pride
And perverse speech
Are the very ways of wickedness that I hate!

The Power of Wisdom

[14]You will find true success when you find Me,
For I have insight into wise plans,
That are designed just for you!
I hold in My hands living understanding,
Courage and strength.
They're all ready and waiting for you!
[15]I empower kings to reign,[a]
And rulers to make laws that are just.
[16]I empower princes to rise and take dominion,
And generous ones to govern the earth.[b]
[17]I will show My love
To those who passionately love Me!
For they will search and search continually
Until they find Me![c]
[18]Unending wealth and glory
Comes to those who discover where I dwell;
The riches of righteousness and
A long, satisfying life will be given to them.[d]
[19]What I impart has greater worth
Than gold and treasure,
And the increase I bring benefits more
Than a windfall of income.
[20]I lead you into the ways of righteousness,
To discover the paths of true justice.

---

a. 8:15 We have been made kings and priestly rulers by the grace of redemption.
b. 8:16 As translated from many Hebrew manuscripts and the Septuagint. Other Hebrew manuscripts have, "and all nobles who govern justly." The word, "nobles," can also be translated, "generous ones."
c. 8:17 Wisdom is not found by the half-hearted. One must love wisdom to gain it. A superficial desire will only yield a superficial knowledge.
d. 8:18 Or, "riches and righteousness." The phrase, "a long, satisfying life," is from the Aramaic.

[21]Those who love Me gain great wealth[a]
And a glorious inheritance,
And I will fill their lives with treasures.

Wisdom in the Beginning

[22]In the beginning I was there,
For God possessed Me,[b]
Even before He created the universe.
[23]From eternity past, I was set in place,
Before the world began.
I was anointed from the beginning.[c]
[24]Before the oceans depths
Were poured out,
And before there were any
Glorious fountains overflowing with water—[d]
I was there, dancing![e]
[25]Even before one mountain had been sculpted
Or one hill raised up,
I was already there, dancing!
[26]When He created the earth, the fields,
Even the first atom of dust,
I was already there.
[27]When He hung the tapestry of the heavens
And stretched out the horizon of the earth,
[28]When the clouds and skies were set in place
And the subterranean fountains
Began to flow strong,

---

a. 8:21 The Aramaic is, "I will leave great hope as an inheritance to My friends."
b. 8:22 The Aramaic and the Septuagint read, "The Lord created Me at the beginning." The Hebrew verb translated here "as possessed" has two basic meanings. One is "acquired" and the other is "created." Poetically, it is a statement that the existence of Wisdom (Christ) was not independent of God at creation, but was manifest and possessed by God as He created all things. Otherwise it would sound like God was without wisdom before He created Him. Jesus is not a created being, but was with the Father from the very beginning.
c. 8:23 The Hebrew word for "anointed" is literally, "poured out" and is often used to describe the anointing oil poured out over a king.
d. 8:24 The Hebrew uses the word, *kabad* or"glory" in describing the fountains. It could be translated, "fountains of glory," or "glorious fountains."
e. 8:24 Many translations have, "I was born (or brought forth)." The Hebrew word for "born" is taken from a word that means, "to kick and twirl" or "dance."

I was already there.
[29]When He set in place the pillars of the earth
And spoke the decrees of the seas,
Commanding the waves so that they
Wouldn't overstep their boundaries—
[30]I was there, close to Creator's side[a]
As His Master Artist.[b]
Daily He was filled with delight in Me,
As I playfully rejoiced before Him![c]
[31]I laughed and played,
So happy with what He had made,
While finding all My delight
In the children of men.[d]

Wisdom Worth Waiting For

[32]So listen, My sons and daughters,
To everything I tell you
For nothing will bring you more joy
Than following My ways.
[33]Listen to My counsel
For My instruction will enlighten you;
You'll be wise not to ignore it!
[34]If you wait at wisdom's doorway[e]—
Longing to hear a word for every day,
Joy breaks forth within you
As you listen for what I'll say.
[35]For the fountain of life pours into you
Every time that you find Me,
And this is the secret of growing in the
Delight and the favor of the Lord!
[36]But those who stumble and miss Me
Will be sorry they did!

---

a. 8:30 See John 1:1.
b. 8:30 Or "Architect."
c. 8:30 The Hebrew word usually translated here as simply, "rejoicing," can also be translated, "joyfully playing," or "laughing."
d. 8:31 What a beautiful picture we find here of Wisdom (Christ) who finds His fulfillment in us. See also Psalm 8:4-9; 16:3; and Ephesians 2:10, 19-22.
e. 8:34 Or, "guard the door of my entrances."

For ignoring what I have to say
Will bring harm to your own soul.
Those who hate Me
Are simply flirting with death![a]

Proverbs 9

Wisdom's Feast

[1]Wisdom[b] has built herself a palace,[c]
Upon seven pillars to keep it secure.[d]
[2]She has made ready a banquet feast
And the sacrifice has been killed.[e]
She has mingled her wine and the table's all set.[f]
[3]She has sent out Her maidens—
Crying out from the high place
Inviting everyone to come
And eat until they're full—
[4]"Whoever wants to know Me
And receive My wisdom,
[5]Come and dine at My table
And drink of My wine.
[6]Lay aside your simple thoughts,
And leave your paths behind;
Agree with My ways, live in My truth,
And righteousness you will find.

a. 8:36 To hate wisdom is not only a sign of stupidity, it is a mark of depravity.
b. 9:1 Lady Wisdom is a poetic personification representing Christ, the wisdom of God (1 Corinthians 1:30). This is a classic form of a synecdoche, a figure of speech in which a part of something stands for the whole thing.
c. 9:1 There is a fascinating word play in the Hebrew text. The verb, "to build" and the word "son" come from the same root. Build is *banah* and son is *ben*. The house that Wisdom is building is a "son." You and I are sons of God that are being built into a spiritual house. There is also a verb in the Hebrew for "hewn" (stones). We are living stones raised up to be His temple. See Psalm 127:1; Hebrews 3:5-6; Matthew 7:24-27; and 16:18.
d. 9:1 The seven pillars of wisdom (plural, "wisdoms") point us to the seven days of creation, the seven spirits of God, and the seven components of heavenly wisdom given in James 3:17-18.
e. 9:2 As translated from the Aramaic. The "sacrifice" points us to Calvary. Wisdom's pillar is a cross. The Hebrew is, "She has prepared her meat."
f. 9:2 Wisdom's "feast" will teach us the ways of God. We feed our hearts on revelation-truth that transforms us; then we implement with wise strategies, the understanding we have learned at the feasting table.

⁷If you try to correct an arrogant cynic,
Expect an angry insult in return;
And if you try to confront an evil man,
Don't be surprised if all you get
Is a slap in the face!
⁸So don't even bother to correct a mocker
For he'll only hate you for it.
But go ahead and correct the wise;
They'll love you even more.ᵃ
⁹Teach a wise man what is right
And he'll grow even wiser!
Instruct the lovers of God
And they'll learn even more!
¹⁰The starting point for acquiring wisdom
Is to be consumed with awe
As you worship Jehovah-God.
To receive the revelation of the Holy One,ᵇ
You must come to the One
Who has living understanding.
¹¹Wisdom will extend your life,
Making every year
More fruitful than the one before.
¹²So it is to your advantage to be wise,
But to ignore the counsel of wisdom
Is to invite trouble into your life.ᶜ

A Spirit Named "Foolish."

¹³There is a spirit named, "Foolish"
Who is boisterous and brash;
She's seductive and restless.
¹⁴And there she sits at the gateway
To the high places,

a. 9:8 See Psalm 141:5.
b. 9:10 Literally, "holy ones."
c. 9:12 The Aramaic adds here: "The liar feeds on the wind and chases fantasies, for he has forsaken what is true, to travel in a barren wilderness; forgetting the right paths, he leaves his own vineyard to walk with thirst and gather nothing." And the Greek Septuagint adds here: "If you forsake folly, you will reign forever. Seek discretion, and your understanding will bring you knowledge."

Proverbs 9

> On her throne overlooking the city.
> [15]She preaches to all who walk by her
> Who are clueless as to what is happening:[a]
> [16]"Come home with me," she invites those
> Who are easily led astray, saying,
> [17]"Illicit sex is the best sex of all!
> Our secret affair will be
> Sweeter than all others![b]
> [18]Little do they know
> When they answer her call
> That she dwells among
> The spirits of the dead,
> And all her guests soon become
> Citizens of hell![c]

Proverbs 10

[1]*The Revelation-Wisdom of Solomon*[d]

> When wisdom comes to a son,
> Joy comes to a father.
> When a son turns from wisdom,
> A mother grieves.

---

a. 9:15 Or, "who are walking straight ahead on their path."

b. 9:17 The Hebrew is literally, "Stolen waters are sweet, and bread eaten in secret is pleasant." This is an obvious metaphor of finding sexual pleasure with someone other than your spouse and trying to get away with it. Finding pleasure in your relationship with your spouse is like drinking from a pure, clean fountain. But stolen water from someone else's fountain is yielding to foolishness. Adultery is always sin.

c. 9:18 Older Aramaic and Septuagint manuscripts add a verse here not found in the Hebrew, "But turn away, linger not in the place, or even look at her. Don't drink from a strange fountain; but abstain and drink not from an alien fountain, so that you will enjoy a long life."

d. 10:1 The title of this section starting with Proverbs 10 indicates a different form. Solomon's 400 sayings of wisdom fill this section, going through Proverbs 22:16. This compilation is an assorted collection of proverbs that is not easily outlined, but profound in its scope.

²Gaining wealth through dishonesty[a]
Is no gain at all,
But honesty brings you a lasting happiness.[b]

³The Lord satisfies the longings of all His lovers[c]
But He withholds from the wicked
What their souls crave.[d]

⁴Slackers will know what it means to be poor,
While the hard worker becomes wealthy.

⁵Know the importance of the season you're in
And a wise son you will be,
But what a waste when an incompetent son
Sleeps through his day of opportunity![e]

⁶The lover of God is enriched beyond belief,
But the evil man only curses his luck.[f]

⁷The reputation of the righteous
Becomes a sweet memorial to him,
While the wicked life only leaves a rotten stench.[g]

⁸The heart of the wise will easily accept instruction,
But the one who does all the talking
Is too busy to listen and learn;
They'll just keep stumbling ahead
Into the mess they created.

⁹The one who walks in integrity[h]
Will experience a fearless confidence in life,
But the one who is devious
Will eventually be exposed.

a. 10:2 Or, "the treasures of wickedness."
b. 10:2 Or, "Righteousness (honesty) delivers you from death."
c. 10:3 Or, "satisfies the souls of the righteous."
d. 10:3 The Aramaic is, "the property of the evil He demolishes."
e. 10:5 Or, "To gather in the summer is to be a wise son, but to sleep through the harvest is a disgrace."
f. 10:6 The Hebrew is quite ambiguous and is literally translated, "the mouth of the wicked covers violence."
g. 10:7 Some Hebrew manuscripts and the Aramaic read, "The name of the wicked will be extinguished."
h. 10:9 Or "innocence." The Aramaic is, "He who walks in perfection walks in hope."

¹⁰The troublemaker always has a clever plan
And won't look you in the eye,
But the one who speaks correction honestly
Can be trusted to make peace.ᵃ
¹¹The teachings of the lovers of God are like
Living truth flowing from the fountain of life,
But the words of the wicked
Hide an ulterior motive.ᵇ

¹²Hatred keeps old quarrels aliveᶜ
But love draws a veil over every insultᵈ
And finds a way to make sin disappear.

¹³Words of wisdom flow from the one
With true discernment,
But to the heartless, words of wisdom
Become like rods beating their backside!

¹⁴Wise men don't divulge all that they know,
But chattering fools blurt out
Words that bring them to the brink of ruin.

¹⁵A rich man's wealth becomes
Like a citadel of strength,ᵉ
But the poverty of the poor
Leaves their security in shambles.
¹⁶The lovers of God earn their wages
For a life of righteousness,
But the wages of the wicked
Are squandered on a life of sin.ᶠ
¹⁷If you readily receive correction

You are walking on the path to life,
But if you reject rebuke
You're guaranteed to go astray.ᵍ

---

a. 10:10 As translated from the Septuagint. The Hebrew is "the babbling fool comes to ruin."
b. 10:11 Or, "hide violence."
c. 10:12 The Aramaic is, "Hatred stirs up judgment."
d. 10:12 Love will cover up offenses against us, but never our own offenses against others.
e. 10:15 Or, "his fortified city."
f. 10:16 Or, "their harvest of wickedness."
g. 10:17 The Aramaic is even more blunt, "Reject rebuke and you're a moron!"

¹⁸The one who hides their hatred
While pretending to be your friend
Is nothing but a liar;
But the one who slanders you behind your back
Proves that he's a fool, never to be trusted.

¹⁹If you keep talking it won't be long
Before you're saying something really wrong;
Prove you're wise from the very start—
Just bite your tongue and be strong!

²⁰The teachings of the godly ones are like pure silver
Bringing words of redemption to others,ᵃ
But the heart of the wicked is corrupt.
²¹The lovers of God feed many with their teachingsᵇ
But the foolish ones starve themselves
For lack of an understanding heart.
²²True enrichment comes
From the blessing of the Lord,
With rest and contentmentᶜ
In knowing that it all comes from Him.

²³The fool finds his fun in doing wrongᵈ
But the wise delight in having discernment.

²⁴The lawless are haunted by their fears
And what they dread will come upon them,ᵉ
But the longings of the lovers of God
Will all be fulfilled.
²⁵The wicked are blown away
By every stormy wind,
But when a catastrophe comes
The lovers of God have a secure anchor.

---

a. 10:20 Or, "the tongue of the just is like choice silver." Silver is a metaphor for redemption.
b. 10:21 The Aramaic is, "The lips of the righteous multiply mercy."
c. 10:22 Or, "with no labor or sorrow attached."
d. 10:23 The word for "fool" is "moron" in the Aramaic.
e. 10:24 This speaks of the consequences of sin. There is a Judge who sees all that we do and will call us to account one day.

[26]To trust a lazy person to get a job done
Will be as irritating as smoke in your eyes—
As enjoyable as a toothache!

[27]To live in the worship and awe of God
Will bring you many years of contented living—
So how could the wicked ever expect
To have a long, happy life?
[28]Lovers of God have a joyful feast of gladness,
But the ungodly see their hopes vanish
Right before their eyes.
[29]The beautiful ways of God are a safe resting place[a]
For those who have integrity,
But to those who work wickedness
The ways of God spell doom.
[30]God's lover can never be greatly shaken,
But the wicked will never inherit
The covenant blessings.[b]

[31]The teachings of the righteous
Are loaded with wisdom,
But the words of the evil
Are crooked and perverse.
[32]Words that bring delight
Pour from the lips of the godly,
But the words of the wicked are duplicitous.

Proverbs 11

Living in Righteousness

[1]To set high standards for someone else[c]
And then not even live up to them yourself,
Is something that God truly hates.
But it pleases Him when we apply
The right standards of measurement.[d]

---

a. 10:29 The Aramaic is, "The way of Jehovah is power to the perfect."

b. 10:30 Or "land." This is a metaphor for all of the covenantal blessings.

c. 11:1 The Hebrew is literally, "scales of deception [false balance]."

d. 11:1 The Hebrew is literally, "a perfect stone." The stone was used as the legitimate weight of balance. Jesus is the Perfect Stone. See Revelation 2:17.

²When you act with presumption,
Convinced that you're right,
Don't be surprised
If you fall flat on your face!
Walking in humility
Helps to make wise decisions.

³Integrity will lead you to success and happiness,
But treachery will destroy your dreams.

⁴When judgment day comes,
All the wealth of the world
Won't help you one bit—
So you'd better be rich in righteousness,
For that's the only thing
That can save you in death.

⁵Those with good character
Walk on a smooth path
With no detour or deviation,
But the wicked keep falling
Because of their own wickedness.
⁶Integrity will keep a good man from falling
But the unbeliever is trapped,
Held captive to his sinful desires.

⁷When an evil man dies, all hope is lost;
For his misplaced confidence goes in the coffin
And gets buried along with him.

⁸Lovers of God are snatched away from trouble,
And the wicked show up in their place!ᵃ

⁹The teachings of hypocrites can destroy you,
But revelation-knowledge
Will rescue the righteous.ᵇ

¹⁰The blessing that rests on the righteous,
Releases strength and favor to the entire city,ᶜ

---

a. 11:8 Haman is a classic example of this principle. See Esther 7:10; 9:24-25.
b. 11:9 Or, "the righteous will be strengthened."
c. 11:10 As translated from the Aramaic and the Septuagint.

But shouts of joy will be heard
When the wicked one dies.
[11]The blessing of favor resting upon the righteous,
Influences a city to lift it higher,[a]
But wicked leaders
Tear it apart by their words.

[12]To quarrel with a neighbor is senseless.[b]
Bite your tongue, be wise and keep quiet!
[13]You can't trust a gossiper with a secret;
They'll just go blab it all;
Put your assurance instead in a trusted friend
For they'll be faithful to keep it in confidence.

[14]People lose their way without wise leadership,
But a nation succeeds and stands in victory
When it has many good counselors to guide it.

[15]The evil man will do harm
When confronted by a righteous man,
Because he hates those who await good news.[c]

[16]A gracious, generous woman will be
Honored with a splendid[d] reputation,
But the woman who hates the truth
Lives surrounded with disgrace,[e]
And men who are cutthroats
Are only after money.[f]
[17]A man of kindness attracts favor
While a cruel man attracts nothing but trouble.[g]

---

a. 11:11 Jesus describes the church as a city. See Matthew 5:14
b. 11:12 Or, "To disparage your neighbor is to be heartless."
c. 11:15 As translated from the Aramaic and the Septuagint. There is a vast difference between this and the Hebrew text, which reads, "You'll be ruined if you cosign for a stranger, and a hater of handshakes will be safe."
d. 11:16, Or "glorious."
e. 11:16 As translated from the older Aramaic and Septuagint texts, but not included in newer Hebrew manuscripts. There is an additional line added by the Aramaic and the Septuagint: "The lazy will lack; the diligent will support themselves financially."
f. 11:16 The Septuagint is, "the diligent obtain wealth."
g. 11:17 The Hebrew text indicates this "trouble" could be physical, related to one's health.

[18]Evil people may get a short-term gain,[a]
But to sow seeds of righteousness
Will bring a true and lasting reward.

[19]A son of righteousness[b]
Experiences the abundant life,
But the one who pursues evil
Hurries to his own death.

[20]The Lord can't stand
The stubborn heart bent toward evil,
But He treasures those
Whose ways are pure.[c]

[21]Assault your neighbor and you will
Certainly be punished,[d]
But God will rescue the children of the godly.

[22]A beautiful woman
Who abandons good morals
Is like a fine gold ring
Dangling from a pig's snout.

[23]True lovers of God are filled with longings
For what is pleasing and good,
But the wicked can only expect doom.

[24]Generosity brings prosperity,
But withholding from charity
Brings poverty.
[25]The one who lives to bless others[e]
Will have blessings heaped upon them,
And the one who pours out his life
To pour out blessings,
Will be saturated with favor!

---

a. 11:18 Or, "wages of deception."
b. 11:19 As translated from one Hebrew manuscript, the Aramaic, and the Septuagint. Most Hebrew manuscripts have: "The one who pursues righteousness."
c. 11:20 Or "wholehearted."
d. 11:21 As translated from the Aramaic and the Targum (a Hebrew-Aramaic commentary).
e. 11:25 The Hebrew is literally, "'the soul of blessing' will grow fat."

²⁶People will curse the business with no ethics,
But the ones with a social conscience
Receives praise from all.^a
²⁷Living your life seeking what is good for others
Brings untold favor,
But the one who wishes evil for others
Will find it coming back on them!
²⁸Keep trusting in your riches and down you'll go!
But the lovers of God rise up
Like flowers in the spring!

²⁹The fool who brings trouble to his own family
Will be cut out of the will,
And he will end up serving a wiser man.
³⁰But a life lived loving God
Bears lasting fruit,
For the one who is truly wise
Wins souls.^b
³¹If the righteous are barely saved
What's in store for all the wicked?^c

Proverbs 12

It's Right to Live for God

¹To learn the truth you must long to be teachable,^d
Or you can despise correction and remain ignorant.

²If your heart is right, favor flows from the Lord,
But a devious heart invites His condemnation.
³You can't expect success by doing what's wrong,
But the lives of His lovers
Are deeply rooted and firmly planted.

---

a. 11:26 The Hebrew is literally, "The one who withholds produce will be cursed, but blessing will be on the head of the one who sells it."
b. 11:30 As translated from the Hebrew. The Aramaic and the Septuagint read, "the souls of violent ones will be removed."
c. 11:31 As translated from the Septuagint. See also 1 Peter 4:18.
d. 12:1 There are times when even the wise need correction, but they will appreciate its value.

[4]The integrity and strength of a virtuous wife[a]
Transforms her husband into an honored king,[b]
But the wife who disgraces her husband
Weakens the strength of his identity.[c]

[5]The lovers of God are filled with good ideas
That are noble and pure,
But the schemes of the sinner
Are crammed with nothing but lies.
[6]The wicked use their words to ambush and accuse,[d]
But the lovers of God speak to defend and protect.
[7]The wicked are taken out, gone for good,
But the godly families shall live on.

[8]Everyone admires a man of principle,
But the one with a corrupt heart is despised.
[9]Just be who you are and work hard for a living,
For that's better than pretending to be important
And starving to death!

[10]A good man takes care of the needs of his pets,
While even the kindest acts of a wicked man
Are still cruel.

[11]Work hard at your job and you'll have what you need,
Fo;r following a get-rich scheme is nothing but a fantasy.
[12]The cravings of the wicked are only for what is evil,[e]
But righteousness is the core motivation
For the lovers of God,
And it keeps them content and flourishing.[f]

---

a. 12:4 There is an amazing Hebrew word used here. It is more commonly used to describe warriors, champions, and mighty ones. Many translations read, "an excellent wife." But the meaning of the Hebrew word *chayil* is better translated, an "army, wealthy, strong, mighty, powerful, with substance, valiant, virtuous, or worthy."

b. 12:4 Or, "an excellent wife is the crown of her husband." By implication, her dignity makes him a king.

c. 12:4 Or, "she is like cancer in his bones." Bones are a metaphor for inner strength, our inner being or identity.

d. 12:6 Or, "lie in wait for blood." This is a figure of speech for accusation.

e. 12:12 As translated from the Septuagint. The Hebrew is, "Thieves crave the loot of other thieves."

f. 12:12 The meaning of the Hebrew text is uncertain.

Proverbs 12

Wisdom Means Being Teachable

[13]The wicked will get trapped by their words
Of gossip, slander, and lies[a];
But for the righteous, honesty is its own defense.
[14]For there is great satisfaction in speaking the truth,
And hard work brings blessings back to you.

[15]A fool is in love with his own opinion,
But wisdom means being teachable.

Learning to Speak Wisely

[16]If you shrug off an insult and refuse to take offense
You demonstrate discretion indeed.[b]
But the fool has a short fuse and will
Immediately let you know he's offended.

[17]Truthfulness marks the righteous,
But the habitual liar can never be trusted.
[18]Reckless words are like the thrusts of a sword:
Cutting remarks meant to stab and to hurt,[c]
But the words of the wise soothe and heal.
[19]Truthful words will stand the test of time,
But one day every lie will be seen for what it is.

[20]Deception fills the hearts of those who plot harm,
But those who promote peace are filled with joy.

[21]Calamity is not allowed to overwhelm the righteous,
But there's nothing but trouble waiting for the wicked.

[22]Live in the truth and keep your promises,
And the Lord will keep delighting in you,
But He detests a liar.

[23]Those who possess wisdom don't feel the need
To impress others with what they know,
But foolish ones make sure their ignorance is on display.

---

a. 12:13 The Hebrew is simply, "sinful words," which imply "gossip, slander, and lies."
b. 12:16 Or, "A shrewd man conceals his shame."
c. 12:18 Implied in the text.

[24]If you want to reign in life,[a]
Don't sit on your hands;
Instead work hard at doing what's right,
For the slacker will end up working
To make someone else succeed.

[25]Anxious fear brings depression,
But a life-giving word of encouragement
Can do wonders to restore joy to the heart.[b]
[26]Lovers of God give good advice to their friends,[c]
But the counsel of the wicked will lead them astray.

[27]A passive person won't even complete a project,[d]
But a passionate person makes good use
Of his time, wealth, and energy.
[28]Abundant life is discovered
By walking in righteousness,
But holding onto your anger
Leads to death.[e]

Proverbs 13

Living Wisely

[1]A wise son or daughter desires a father's discipline,
But the know-it-all never listens to correction.
[2]The words of the wise are kind and easy to swallow,
But the unbeliever just wants to pick a fight and argue.
[3]Guard your words and you'll guard your life,

a. 12:24 The Hebrew word for "reign" is *mashal*, and is the title of the book—Proverbs! See introduction and the footnote on 1:1.
b. 12:25 This insightful proverb can also be translated, "Stop worrying! Think instead of what brings you gladness." Our focus must never be on what we can't change, but on the everlasting joy we have in Christ. Sometimes we have to find the life-giving word of encouragement rising up in our own hearts. This is the secret of finding perpetual encouragement by the Word that lives in us.
c. 12:26 As translated from older Aramaic manuscripts. The Hebrew is uncertain.
d. 12:27 Implied in the text, and paraphrased from an uncertain Hebrew phrase. An alternate translation would be, "A lazy person won't get to roast the game he caught, but the wealth of a diligent person is precious."
e. 12:28 As translated from the Septuagint and the Aramaic. The Hebrew is uncertain.

But if you don't control your tongue,
It will ruin everything.

[4]The slacker wants it all but ends up with nothing.
But the hard worker ends up with all that he longed for.

[5]Lovers of God hate what is phony and false,
But the wicked are full of shame[a]
And have no confidence.
[6]Righteousness is like a shield of protection,
Guarding those who keep their integrity,
But sin is the downfall of the wicked.

[7]One simply pretends to be rich, but is poor.
Another pretends to be very poor, but is quite rich.[b]
[8]The self-assurance of the rich is their money,[c]
But people don't kidnap and extort the poor!

[9]The virtues of God's lovers
Shine brightly in the darkness,
But the flickering lamp of the ungodly
Will be extinguished.
[10]Wisdom opens your heart to receive wise counsel,
But pride closes your ears to advice,
And gives birth to only quarrels and strife.

[11]Wealth quickly gained is quickly wasted[d]—
Easy come, easy go!
But if you gradually gain wealth,
You will watch it grow.
[12]When hope's dream seems to drag on and on
The delay can be depressing,
But when at last your dream comes true,
Life's sweetness will satisfy your soul.[e]

---

a. 13:5 The Hebrew word used here is quite interesting. It literally means, "to cause a stink," or, "emit an odor." This is a figure of speech for what is shameful.

b. 13:7 It is never godly to be a phony. It's always better to be who you are and avoid pretense.

c. 13:8 The Aramaic is, "The salvation of the soul is a man's true wealth."

d. 13:11 Or, "Wealth gained by fraud will dwindle."

e. 13:12 Or, "It is a tree of life."

¹³Despise the Word, will you?
Then you'll pay the price and it won't be pretty!
But the one who honors the Father's holy instructions
Will be rewarded.
¹⁴When the lovers of God teach you truth
A fountain of life opens up within you,
And their wise instruction will deliver you
From the ways of death.
¹⁵Everyone admires a wise, sensible person,
But the treacherous walk on the path of ruin.ª
¹⁶Everything a wise and shrewd man does
Comes from a source of revelation-knowledge,ᵇ
But the behavior of a fool puts foolishness on parade!ᶜ

¹⁷An undependable messenger causes a lot of trouble,
But the trustworthy and wise messengers
Release healing wherever they go.ᵈ

¹⁸Poverty and disgrace comes to the one
Who refuses to hear criticism,ᵉ
But the one who is easy to correct
Is on the path of honor.
¹⁹When God fulfills your longings,
Sweetness fills your soul,
But the wicked refuse to turn from darkness
To see their desires come to pass.ᶠ
²⁰If you want to grow in wisdom,
Then spend time with the wise!
Walk with the wicked,
And you'll eventually become just like them!

²¹Calamity chases the sin-chaser,
But prosperity pursues the God-lover.

---

a. 13:15 As translated from the Aramaic and the Septuagint. The Hebrew is uncertain.
b. 13:16 Or, "A wise person thinks ahead."
c. 13:16 The implication is that the fool is unable to finish anything he begins.
d. 13:17 God's sons and daughters are peacemakers, healers, and faithful deliverers for others.
e. 13:18 As translated from the Hebrew. The Septuagint is, "Instruction removes poverty and disgrace."
f. 13:19 Implied by the Hebrew parallelism of the text.

[22]The benevolent man leaves an inheritance
That endures to his children's children,
But the wealth of the wicked
Is treasured up for the righteous.
[23]The lovers of God will live a long life
And get to enjoy their wealth,
But the ungodly will suddenly perish.[a]

[24]If you withhold correction and punishment[b]
From your children,
You demonstrate a lack of true love,
So prove your love and be prompt to punish them.[c]
[25]The lovers of God will have more than enough,
But the wicked will always lack what they crave.

Proverbs 14

The House of Wisdom

[1]Every wise woman encourages and
Builds up her family,
But a foolish woman—over time—
Will tear it down by her own actions.

[2]Lovers of truth follow the right path
Because of their wonderment and worship of God,
But the devious display their disdain for Him!
[3]The words of a proud fool
Will all come back to haunt him.
But the words of the wise
Will become a shield of protection around them.

---

a. 13:23 As translated from the Septuagint. The Hebrew is, "In the fallow ground of the poor there is abundance of food, but injustice sweeps it away." The Aramaic is, "Those who don't find the way of life destroy many years of wealth and some are utterly destroyed." There is a vast difference in the three translations. The translator has chosen to follow the Septuagint.
b. 13:24 Or, "Sparing the rod."
c. 13:24 Or, "The one who spares the rod hates his child."

⁴The only clean stable is an empty stable,
So if you want the work of an ox
And enjoy an abundant harvest,
You'll have a mess or two to clean up!

⁵An honest witness will never lie,
But a deceitful witness lies with every breath.

⁶The intellectually arrogant seek for wisdom
But they never seem to discover
What they claim they're looking for.
For revelation-knowledge flows to the one
Who hungers for understanding.

⁷The words of the wise
Are like weapons of knowledge.ª
So if you need wise counsel,
Stay away from the fool.
⁸For the wisdom of the wise
Will keep life on the right track,
While the fool only deceives himself
And refuses to face reality.
⁹Fools mock the need for repentanceᵇ
While the favor of God rests upon all His lovers.

¹⁰Don't expect anyone else to fully understand
Both the bitterness and the joys
Of all you experience in your life.

¹¹The household of the wicked is soon torn apart
While the family of the righteous flourishes.

¹²You can rationalize it all you want—
And justify the path of error you have chosen,
But you'll find out in the end,
That you took the road to destruction.

---

a. 14:7 As translated from Aramaic.
b. 14:9 Or, "Fools mock guilt," or, "guilt offering." The Septuagint is, "The house of the transgressor owes purification."

¹³Superficial laughter can hide a heavy heart,
But when the laughter ends,
The pain resurfaces.

¹⁴Those who turn from the truth
Get what they deserve,
But a good person receives a sweet reward.^a

¹⁵A gullible person will believe anything,
But a sensible person will confirm the facts.
¹⁶A wise person is careful in all things
And turns quickly from evil,
While the impetuous fool
Moves ahead with overconfidence.
¹⁷An impulsive person has a short fuse
And can ruin everything,
But the wise show self-control.^b
¹⁸The naïve demonstrate a lack of wisdom,
But the lovers of wisdom are crowned
With revelation-knowledge.

¹⁹Evil ones will pay tribute to good people,
And eventually come to be servants of the godly.^c

²⁰The poor are disliked even by their neighbors,
But everyone wants to get close to the wealthy.
²¹It's a sin to despise one
Who is less fortunate than you,^d
But when you are kind to the poor,
You will prosper and be blessed.

²²Haven't you noticed how evil schemers
Always wander astray?

a. 14:14 As translated from Hebrew manuscripts. The Aramaic is, "a good man will be filled from the awe of his soul."
b. 14:17 As translated from the Aramaic. The Hebrew is, "And a crafty schemer is hated."
c. 14:19 Implied in the text. The Hebrew is literally, "They will come [or 'bow'] at the gates of the righteous."
d. 14:21 Implied in the Hebrew parallelism. The Hebrew is literally, "your neighbor."

But kindness and truth come to those
Who make plans to be pure in all their ways.[a]

²³If you work hard at what you do,
Great abundance will come to you;
But merely talking about getting rich
While living only to pursue your pleasures,[b]
Brings you face to face with poverty.[c]
²⁴The true net worth of the wise[d]
Is the wealth that wisdom imparts,
But the way of life for the fool is his foolishness.[e]

²⁵Speak the truth and you'll save souls;
But in the spreading of lies, treachery thrives.

²⁶Confidence and strength flood the hearts
Of the lovers of God who live in awe of Him,
And their devotion provides their children
With a place of shelter and security.[f]
²⁷To worship God in wonder and awe
Opens a fountain of life within you,
Empowering you to escape death's domain.[g]

²⁸A king glories in the number of his loyal followers,
But a dwindling population
Spells ruin for any leader.

²⁹When your heart overflows with understanding,
You'll be very slow to get angry,
But if you have a quick temper,
Your impatience will be quickly seen by all.

a. 14:22 Both the Aramaic and the Septuagint insert a verse here that is not found in the Hebrew: "The followers of evil don't understand mercy and faith, but you'll find kindness and faith with those who do good."
b. 14:23 As translated from the Septuagint.
c. 14:23 There is an additional verse found here in the Aramaic that is missing from the Hebrew text: "The Lord Jehovah heals every sickness, but evil speaking makes you sick [harms you]."
d. 14:24 Or, "the crown of the wise."
e. 14:24 The Aramaic word here for "foolishness" is "insanity."
f. 14:26 To live as a passionate lover of God will bring benefit even to your children.
g. 14:27 Or, "Empowering you to turn from the deadly snares."

[30]A tender, tranquil heart will make you healthy,[a]
But jealousy can make you sick.

[31]Insult your Creator, will you?
That's exactly what you do every time
That you oppress the powerless![b]
Showing kindness to the poor
Is equal to honoring your Maker.

[32]The wicked are crushed by every calamity,
But the lovers of God find a strong hope,
Even in the time of death.[c]

[33]Wisdom soothes the heart
Of the one with living-understanding,
But the heart of the fool just stockpiles stupidity.

[34]A nation is exalted by
The righteousness of its people,
But sin heaps disgrace upon the land.

[35]A wise and faithful servant receives
Promotion from the king,
But the one who acts disgracefully
Gets to taste the anger of the king![d]

Proverbs 15

Wisdom Far Better than Wickedness

[1]Respond gently when you are confronted
And you'll defuse the rage of another;
Responding with sharp, cutting words[e]

---

a. 14:30 Implied in the text. The Hebrew reads, "A heart of healing is the life of the flesh."
b. 14:31 Or, "slander the poor." Every human being is made in God's image, including the poor.
c. 14:32 Our "strong hope" is that our life will continue in the presence of God in the resurrection glory. Both the Septuagint and the Aramaic read quite differently: "But the one who trusts in his integrity is righteous."
d. 14:35 As translated from the Hebrew. The Septuagint reads, "and by his good behavior, shame is removed."
e. 15:1 Or, "painful words."

Will only make it worse.
Don't you know that being angry
Can ruin the testimony
Of even the wisest of men[a]?

[2]When wisdom speaks,
Understanding becomes attractive.
But the words of the fool makes
Their ignorance look laughable.[b]

[3]The eyes of the Lord are everywhere[c]
And He takes note of everything that happens;
He watches over His lovers,
And He also sees the wickedness of the wicked.

[4]When you speak healing words,
You offer others fruit from the Tree of Life,
But unhealthy, negative words do nothing
But crush their hopes.[d]

[5]You're stupid to mock the instruction of a father,
But welcoming correction will make you brilliant![e]

[6]There is power in the house of the righteous,[f]
But the house of the wicked
Is filled with trouble,
No matter how much money they have.

[7]When wisdom speaks
Revelation-knowledge is released,[g]
But finding true wisdom
In the words of a fool is futile.

---

a. 15:1 This is found only in the Septuagint.
b. 15:2 The Aramaic reads, "the mouth of fools vomit a curse."
c. 15:3 The eyes of the Lord can also be a metaphor for His prophets.
d. 15:4 Or, "Perverse words are the crushing of the spirit."
e. 15:5 The Septuagint adds a verse that is not found in the Hebrew: "In great righteousness, there is great strength, but the ungodly will one day perish from the earth."
f. 15:6 As translated from the Septuagint and the Aramaic. The Hebrew changes the concept of "power" to "prosperity." Both concepts are valid.
g. 15:7 Or, "is scattered like seed."

⁸It is despicable to the Lord
When people use the worship of the Almighty
As a cloak for their sin,ᵃ
But every prayer of His godly lovers
Is pleasing to His heart.
⁹The Lord detests the lifestyle of the wicked,
But He loves those who pursue purity.ᵇ
¹⁰Severe punishment awaits the one
Who turns away from the truth;
And those who rebel against correction
Will die.

¹¹Even hell itself holds no secrets
From the Lord God,
For all is exposed before His eyes.
And so much more
The heart of every human being!

¹²The know-it-all never esteems
The one who tries to correct him;
He refuses to seek good advice from the wise.ᶜ

Living an Ascended Life

¹³A cheerful heart puts a smile on your face,
But a broken heart leads to depression.
¹⁴Lovers of Godᵈ hunger after truth,
But those without understanding
Feast on foolishness and don't even realize it.
¹⁵Everything seems to go wrong
When you feel weak and depressed,
But when you choose to be cheerful
Every day will bring you
More and more joy and fullness!ᵉ

a. 15:8 Or, "the sacrifice of the wicked." That is, worshipping God with a wicked heart, only to hide sin. Our yielded heart must be the sacrifice we offer to God.
b. 15:9 The Aramaic reads, "He shows mercy to the one who practices righteousness."
c. 15:12 Another way to say this is, "The one who hates authority has no love for being taught."
d. 15:14 The Aramaic read, "the upright."
e. 15:15 The Septuagint reads quite differently, "and the good (heart) is always calm."

¹⁶It's so much better to live simply—
Surrounded in holy awe and worship of God,
Than to have great wealth
With a home full of trouble.
¹⁷It's so much better to have a kind, loving family
Even with little,
Than to have great wealth
With nothing but hatred and strife all around you.ᵃ

¹⁸A touchy, hot-tempered man picks a fight,
But the calm, patient man knows how to silence strife.
¹⁹Nothing seems to work rightᵇ for the lazy man,
But life seems smooth and easy
When your heart is virtuous.

²⁰When a son learns wisdom,
A father's heart is glad,
But the man who shamesᶜ his mother
Is a foolish son.

²¹The senseless fool treats life like a joke,
But the one with living-understanding
Makes good choices.

²²Your plans will fall apart right in front of you
If you fail to get good advice,
But if you first seek out multiple counselors,
You'll watch your plans succeed.

²³Everyone enjoys giving great advice,
But how delightful it is
To say the right thing at the right time!

²⁴The life-path of the prudent
Lifts them progressively heavenward,
Delivering them from the death spiral
That keeps tugging them downward.

---

a. 15:17 Or, "Better to have a meal of vegetables surrounded with love and grace, than a
fattened ox where there is hatred."
b. 15:19 Or, "The way is blocked with thorns."
c. 15:20 Or "despises."

²⁵The Lord champions the widow's cause,ᵃ
But watch Him as He smashes down
The houses of the haughty!

²⁶The Lord detests wicked ways of thinking,ᵇ
But He enjoys lovely and delightful words!

²⁷The one who puts earning money above his family
Will have trouble at home,
But those who refuse to exploit others
Will live in peace.ᶜ

²⁸An honorable man thinks carefully before he speaks,
But the careless blurt out wicked words
Meant to cause harm.

²⁹The Lord doesn't respond to the wicked,
But He's moved to answer the prayers
Of His godly lovers.

³⁰Eyes that focus upon what is beautifulᵈ
Bring joy to your heart,
And hearing a good report refreshes
And strengthens the inner being.ᵉ

³¹Accepting constructive criticism
Opens your heart to the path of life,
Making you right at home among the wise.
³²Refusing constructive criticism shows
You have no interest in improving your life,
For revelation-insight only comes
As you accept correction,
And the wisdom that it brings.
³³The source of revelation-knowledge is found
As you fall down in surrender before the Lord.

---

a. 15:25 Or, "The Lord maintains the boundaries of the widow."
b. 15:26 Or, "the thoughts of the wicked."
c. 15:27 Implied in the text.
d. 15:30 As translated from the Septuagint. The Hebrew is, "The light of the eyes brings joy."
e. 15:30 The Hebrew is literally, "makes fat your bones." Bones picture our inner being.

Don't expect to see Shekinah glory[a]
Until the Lord sees your sincere humility!

Proverbs 16

Wisdom Exalts God

[1]Go ahead and make all the plans you want,
But it's the Lord who will ultimately direct your steps.[b]
[2]We are all in love with our own opinions,
Convinced they're correct,
But the Lord is in the midst of us,[c]
Testing and probing our every motive.
[3]Before you do anything
Put your trust totally in God and not in yourself[d]—
Then every plan you make will succeed!

[4]The Lord works everything together
To accomplish His purpose[e];
Even the wicked are included in His plans—
He sets them aside for the day of disaster!

[5]Exalting yourself is disgusting to the Lord,
For pride attracts His punishment—
And you can count on that!

[6]You can avoid evil through surrendered worship
And the fear of God,
For the power of His faithful love
Removes sin's guilt and grip over you!

[7]When the Lord is pleased
With the decisions you've made,
He activates grace to turn enemies into friends.

---

a. 15:33 The Hebrew word is *kabod*, which is translated 156 times as "glory."
b. 16:1 As translated from the Septuagint. The Hebrew and Aramaic read, "The Lord gives the right reply."
c. 16:2 Or, "in the midst of spirits."
d. 16:3 Or, "Commit your business to God."
e. 16:4 Or, "for its answer."

[8]It is better to have little
With a heart that loves justice,
Than to be rich and not have God on your side.

[9]Within your heart, you can make plans for your future,
But the Lord chooses the steps you take to get there.

Living Like a King

[10]A king speaks the revelation of truth,
So he must be extraordinarily careful
In the decrees that he makes.
[11]The Lord expects you to be fair in every business deal
For He is the One who sets
The standards for righteousness![a]
[12]Kings and leaders despise wrongdoing,
For the true authority to rule and reign
Is built on a foundation of righteousness.
[13]Kings and leaders love to hear godly counsel,
And they will love those who will tell them the truth.
[14]The anger of a king releases the messenger of death,[b]
But a wise person will know how to pacify his wrath.
[15]Life-giving light streams from the presence of a king,[c]
And his favor is showered upon those who please him.

[16]Everyone wants gold, but wisdom's worth[d] is far greater!
Silver is sought after, but a heart of understanding
Yields a greater return!

[17]Repenting from evil places you
On the highway of holiness;
Protect purity and you protect your life![e]
[18]Your boast becomes a prophecy

---

a. 16:11 Or, "Honesty with scales and balances is the way of the Lord, for all the stones in the bag are established by Him."
b. 16:14 See 1 Kings 2:25, 29-34, and 46.
c. 16:15 The Septuagint reads, "The king's son is in the light of life."
d. 16:16 The Septuagint is, "nests of wisdom."
e. 16:17 There are two proverbs inserted here in the Septuagint that are not found in the Hebrew or Aramaic: "Receive instruction and you'll be prosperous; and he that listens to correction shall be made wise. He that guards his ways preserves his own soul; and he that loves his life will watch his words."

Of a future failure;
The higher you lift up yourself in pride,[a]
The harder you'll fall in disgrace!
[19]It's better to be meek and lowly and live among the poor,
Than to live high and mighty among the rich and famous!

[20]One skilled in business discovers prosperity,
But the one who trusts in God is blessed beyond belief!

Walking with Wisdom

[21]The one with a wise heart is called, "discerning,"
And speaking sweetly to others
Makes your teaching even more convincing.
[22]Wisdom is a deep well of understanding
Opened up within you
As a fountain of life for others,
But it's senseless to try to instruct a fool.
[23]Winsome words pour from a heart of wisdom,
Adding value to all you teach.
[24]Nothing is more appealing
Than speaking beautiful, life-giving words,
For they release sweetness to our soul
And inner healing to our spirit.[b]

[25]Before every person there is a path
That seems like the right one to take,
But it leads them straight to hell![c]

[26]Life motivation comes
From the deep longings of the heart,
And the passion to see them fulfilled
Urges you onward.[d]

[27]A wicked scoundrel wants to dig up dirt on others,
Only to spread slander and shred their reputation.
[28]A twisted person spreads rumors;
A whispering gossip ruins good friendships.

---

a. 16:18 Or "overconfidence."
b. 16:24 Or, "healing to the bones." Bones become a metaphor of our inner being.
c. 16:25 As translated from the Septuagint. The Hebrew is, "the ways of death."
d. 16:26 The meaning of the Hebrew in this verse is uncertain.

²⁹A vicious criminal can be persuasive,
Enticing others to join him as partners in crime,
But he leads them all down a despicable path.
³⁰It's so easy to tell when a wicked man
Is hatching some crooked scheme:
It's written all over his face!
His looks betray him as he gives birth to his sin.

³¹Old age with wisdom will crown you
With dignity and honor,
For it takes a lifetime of righteousness
To acquire it.^a

³²Do you want to be a mighty warrior?
It's better to be known as one who is patient and slow to anger.^b
Do you want to conquer a city?
Rule over your temper
Before you attempt to rule a city.^c

³³We may toss the coin and roll the dice
But God's will is greater than "luck."^d

Proverbs 17

Wisdom's Virtues

¹A simple, humble life, with peace and quiet
Is far better than an opulent lifestyle with nothing
But quarrels and strife at home!

²A wise, intelligent servant will be honored above
A shameful son;
He'll even end up having a portion left to him
In his master's will.

---

a. 16:31 Or, "Gray hair is a crown of splendor." In the Hebrew culture, the old are honored above all, especially if they acquired wisdom. See Leviticus 19:32.
b. 16:32 The Septuagint is, "It's better to be forgiving than strong."
c. 16:32 Implied in the text.
d. 16:33 Or, "Into the center, the lot is cast, and from Jehovah is all its judgment."

[3]In the same way gold and silver are refined by fire,
The Lord purifies your heart
By the tests and trials of life.

[4]Those eager to embrace evil listen to slander,
For a liar loves to listen to lies.

[5]Mock the poor, will you?
You insult your Creator every time you do!
If you make fun of others' misfortune,
You better watch out—your punishment is on its way!

[6]Grandparents have the crowning glory of life—
Grandchildren! And it's only proper for children
To take pride in their parents.[a]

[7]It is not proper for a leader to lie and deceive,
And don't expect excellent words
To be spoken by a fool.[b]

[8]Wise instruction is like a costly gem;
It turns the impossible into success.[c]

[9]Love overlooks the mistakes of others,
But dwelling on the failures of others devastates friendships.

[10]One word of correction breaks open
A teachable heart,
But a fool can be corrected a hundred times,
And he still doesn't know what hit him.
[11]Rebellion thrives in an evil man,
So a messenger of vengeance[d]
Will be sent to punish him.[e]
[12]It's safer to meet a grizzly bear robbed of her cubs
Than to confront a reckless fool.

---

a. 17:6 Or "fathers." There is an additional verse inserted here that is found in the Septuagint:
"A whole world of riches belongs to the faithful, but the unfaithful don't even get a cent."
b. 17:7 Here are two absurd things: to find a fool in leadership and to have a leader in foolishness.
c. 17:8 "Instruction" is taken from the Aramaic. The Hebrew reads, "bribe."
d. 17:11 Or, "merciless angels."
e. 17:11 This could mean an evil spirit, or calamities and sorrows.

¹³The one who returns evil for good
Can expect to be treated the same way
For the rest of his life!ª

¹⁴Don't be one who is quick to quarrel,
For an argument is hard to stop,
And you never know how it will end,
So don't even start down that road!ᵇ

¹⁵There is nothing God hates more
Than condemning the one who is innocent
And acquitting the one who is guilty!

¹⁶Why pay tuition to educate a fool?
For He has no intention of acquiring true wisdom.

¹⁷A dear friend will love you no matter what,
And a family sticks together
Through all kinds of trouble.

¹⁸It's stupid to run up bills
You'll never be able to pay,
Or to cosign for the loan of your friend.
Save yourself the trouble
And don't do either one.ᶜ

¹⁹If you love to argue
Then you must be in love with sin,
For the boasterᵈ
Is only asking for trouble.

²⁰The one with a perverse heart
Never has anything good to say,ᵉ

---

a. 17:13 Or, "evil will haunt his house."
b. 17:14 The Aramaic for this verse reads, "To shed blood provokes the judgment of a ruler."
c. 17:18 Implied by the text.
d. 17:19 Or, "He who builds a high gate." The gate becomes a picture of the mouth. This is a figure of speech for proud boasting.
e. 17:20 Or, "can expect calamity."

And the chronic liar
Tumbles into constant trouble.

²¹Parents of a numskull will have many sorrows,
For there's nothing about his lifestyle
That will make them proud.

²²A joyful, cheerful heart
Brings healing to both body and soul,
But the one whose heart is crushed
Struggles with sickness and depression.

²³When you take a secret bribe, your actions
Reveal your true character
For you pervert the ways of justice.

²⁴Even the face of a wise man shows his intelligence,
But the wandering eyes of a fool
Will look for wisdom everywhere—
Except right in front of his nose.

²⁵A father grieves over the foolishness of his child,
And bitter sorrow fills his mother.

²⁶It's horrible to persecute a holy lover of God,
Or to strike an honorable man for his integrity!

²⁷Can you bridle your tongue
When your heart is under pressure?
That's how you show that you are wise.
An understanding heart keeps you
Cool, calm, and collected,
No matter what you're facing.
²⁸For even when a fool bites his tongue,[a]
He's considered wise;
So shut your mouth when you are provoked—
It makes you look smart.

---

a. 17:28 The Septuagint is, "When an unthinking man asks a question."

Proverbs 18

Wisdom Gives Life

[1]An unfriendly person isolates himself
And seems to care only about his own issues,
For his contempt of sound judgment
Makes him a recluse.[a]

[2]Senseless people find no pleasure
In acquiring true wisdom,
For all they want to do is
Impress you with what they know.

[3]An ungodly man is always cloaked with disgrace
As dishonor and shame are his companions.[b]

[4]Words of wisdom[c] are like a fresh flowing brook,
Like deep waters that spring forth from within
Bubbling up inside the one with understanding.

[5]It is atrocious when judges show favor to the guilty
And deprive the innocent of justice.

[6]A senseless man jumps headfirst into an argument;
He's just asking for a beating for his reckless words.[d]
[7]A fool has a big mouth that only gets him into trouble,
And he'll pay the price for what he says.

[8]The words of a gossip merely
Reveal the wounds of his own soul,[e]
And his slander penetrates
Into the innermost being.

[9]The one who is too lazy to look for work
Is the same one who wastes his life away.

---

a. 18:1 There are alternate possible translations of this verse in the Hebrew-Aramaic: "An idle man meditates on his lusts, and mocks at wise instruction."
b. 18:3 Implied in the text.
c. 18:4 Or, "Words that touch the heart."
d. 18:6 The Aramaic is, "his rash words call for death."
e. 18:8 Scholars are somewhat uncertain about an exact translation of this phrase. The Aramaic is, "The words of a lazy man lead him to fear and evil."

[10]The character of God is a tower of strength[a]
For the lovers of God delight to run into His heart,
And be exalted on high.

[11]The rich, in their conceit, imagine that their wealth
Is enough to protect them;
It becomes their confidence in a day of trouble.[b]

[12]A man's heart is the proudest
When his downfall is nearest,
For he won't see glory until the Lord sees humility.

[13]Listen before you speak, for to speak
Before you've heard the facts
Will bring humiliation!

[14]The will to live sustains you when you're sick,[c]
But depression crushes courage
And leaves you unable to cope.

[15]The spiritually hungry
Are always ready to learn more,
For their hearts are eager to discover new truths.

[16]Would you like to meet a very important person?
Take a generous gift and it will do wonders
To gain entrance into his presence.

[17]There are two sides to every story.
The first one to speak sounds true
Until you hear the other side,
And they set the record straight.[d]

[18]A coin toss[e] resolves a dispute,
And can put an argument to rest
Between formidable opponents.

---

a. 18:10 The Hebrew word, *migdal* for "tower of strength," is a homonym that can also be translated, "pyramidal bed of flowers."
b. 18:11 The Aramaic is, "The wealth of the rich is a strong city, and its glory casts a broad shadow."
c. 18:14 The Septuagint is, "A wise servant can calm a man's anger."
d. 18:17 The text implies that a legal testimony in a courtroom seems to be correct until cross-examination begins.
e. 18:18 The Hebrew is, "casting lots."

[19]It is easier to conquer a strong city
Than to win back a friend that you've offended;
Their walls go up, making it nearly impossible
To win them back.[a]

[20]Sharing words of wisdom
Are satisfying to your inner being.
It encourages you to know that you've
Changed someone else's life.[b]
[21]Your words are so weighty that
They have power to bring life or release death,
And the talkative person
Will reap the consequences.

[22]When a man finds a wife,
He has found a treasure!
For she is the gift of God
To bring him joy and pleasure!
But the one who divorces a good woman
Loses what is good from his house.[c]
To choose an adulteress
Is both stupid and ungodly![d]

[23]The poor plead for help from the rich,
But all they get in return is a harsh response.
[24]Some friendships don't last for long,[e]
But there is one loving Friend
Who is joined to your heart[f]
Closer than any other!

---

a. 18:19 Or, "A brother supported by a brother is like a high, strong city. They hold each other up like the bars of a fortress."
b. 18:20 Or, "A man's belly is filled with the fruits of his mouth, and by the harvest of his lips he will be satisfied."
c. 18:22 This reference to divorce is not found in the Hebrew text, but is included in both the Aramaic and the Septuagint.
d. 18:22 This is not included in the Hebrew or Aramaic, but is found in the Septuagint.
e. 18:24 Or, "A man with too many friends may be broken to pieces."
f. 18:24 The Hebrew word used here can be translated, "joined together," "stick close," "to cleave," "to pursue," or "to overtake."

Chapter 19

Wisdom Exalted

[1]It's better to be honest even if it leads to poverty
Than to live as a dishonest fool.

[2]The best way to live is with revelation-knowledge,
For without it, you'll grow impatient
And run right into error.[a]

[3]There are some people who ruin their own lives
And then blame it all on God.

[4]Being wealthy means having lots of "friends,"
But the poor can't keep the ones they have.

[5]Perjury won't go unpunished,
And liars will get all that they deserve.

[6]Everyone wants to be close to the rich and famous,
But a generous person has all the friends he wants!
[7]When a man is poor, even his family has no use for him;
How much more will his "friends" avoid him—
For though he begs for help, they won't respond.[b]

[8]Do yourself a favor and love wisdom;
Learn all you can,
Then watch your life flourish and prosper!

[9]Tell lies and you're going to get caught,
And the habitual liar is doomed!

[10]It doesn't seem right when you see a fool
Living in the lap of luxury,
Or a prideful servant ruling over princes.

[11]A wise person demonstrates patience,
For mercy[c] means holding your tongue.

---

a. 19:2 Or "sin."
b. 19:7 The Aramaic and the Septuagint adds a sentence not found in the Hebrew: "The one who is malicious with his words is not to be trusted."
c. 19:11 The word "mercy: (merciful) is found only in the Septuagint.

When you are insulted.
Be quick to forgive and forget it,
For you are virtuous
When you overlook an offense

[12]The rage of a king is like the roar of a lion,
But his sweet favor
Is like a gentle, refreshing rain.

[13]A rebellious son breaks a father's heart,
And a nagging wife can drive you crazy!

[14]You can inherit houses
And land from your parents,
But a good[a] wife only comes
As a gracious gift from God!

[15]Go ahead—be lazy and passive,
But you'll go hungry if you live that way!

[16]Honor God's holy instructions
And life will go well for you,
But if you despise His ways
And choose your own plans, you will die.

[17]Every time you give to the poor,
You make a loan to the Lord.
Don't worry—you'll be repaid in full
For all the good you've done!

[18]Don't be afraid to discipline your children
While they're still young enough to learn.
Don't indulge your children
Or be swayed by their protests.

[19]A hot-tempered man
Has to pay the price for his anger.[b]

---

a. 19:14 Literally, "prudent" or "understanding" wife.
b. 19:19 There is an implication in the Hebrew that he will get into legal trouble. An alternate translation of this verse could be: "An evil-minded man will be injured; if you rescue him his anger will only intensify."

If you bail him out once,
You'll do it a dozen times.

²⁰Listen well to wise counsel
And be willing to learn from correction,
So that by the end of your life,
You'll be known for your wisdom.

²¹A person may have many ideas
Concerning God's plan for their life,
But only the designs of His purpose
Will succeed in the end.

²²A man is charming when he displays
Tender mercies to others.
And a lover of God who is poor and
Promises nothing is better than a rich liar
Who never keeps his promises.ᵃ

²³When you live a life of abandoned love,
Surrendered before the awe of God,
Here's what you'll experience:
Abundant life! Continual protection!ᵇ
And complete satisfaction!

²⁴There are some people who pretend they're hurt—
Deadbeats who won't even work
To feed themselves!ᶜ

²⁵If you punish the insolent
Who don't know any better,
They will learn not to mock.
But if you correct a wise man,
He will grow even wiser.

²⁶Kids who mistreat their parents are an
Embarrassment to their family

---

a. 19:22 Implied in the text.
b. 19:23 Or, "You will not be remembered for evil."
c. 19:24 Or, "The lazy man buries his fork in his plate, and won't even lift it up to his mouth."

And a public disgrace.
[27]So, listen, my child, don't reject correction or
You'll certainly wander from the ways of truth.[a]

[28]A corrupt witness makes a mockery of justice
For the wicked will never play by the rules.[b]
[29]Judgment is waiting for those who mock the truth,
And foolish living invites a beating.

Chapter 20

Are You Living Wisely?

[1]A drunkard is obnoxious, loud, and argumentative;
You're a fool to get intoxicated with strong drink.

[2]The rage of a king is like the roar of a lion,
Do you really want to go and make him angry?

[3]A person of honor[c] will put an argument to rest;
Only the stupid want to pick a fight.

[4]If you're too lazy to plant seed,
It's too bad when you have no harvest
On which to feed.[d]

[5]A man of deep understanding
Will give good advice,
Drawing it out from the well within.

[6]Many will tell you they're your loyal friends,
But who can find one who is truly trustworthy?

[7]The lovers of God will walk in integrity,
And their children are fortunate to have
Godly parents as their examples!

---

a. 19:27 Or, "Stop listening to instruction that contradicts what you know is truth."
b. 19:28 Or, "The heart of the wicked feeds on evil."
c. 20:3 Or, "It is the glory of a man." It's better to keep a friend than to win a fight.
d. 20:4 The Aramaic and the Septuagint read: "Rebuke a lazy man and he still has no shame, yet watch him go beg at harvest time."

⁸A righteous king sits on his judgment seat;
He scatters evil away from his kingdom
By his wise discernment.

⁹Which one of us can truly say:
"I am free from sin in my life,
For my heart is clean and pure?"^a

¹⁰Mark it down: God hates it
When you demonstrate a double standard,
One for them and one for you.

¹¹Every child shows what they're really like
By how they act—
You can discern their character—
Whether they are pure or perverse.

¹²Lovers of God have been given eyes
To see with spiritual discernment,
And ears to hear from God.

¹³If you spend all your time sleeping, you'll grow poor,^b
So wake up, sleepyhead; don't sleep on the job,
And then there will be plenty of food on your table.

¹⁴The buyer says, as he haggles over the price,
"That's junk; it's worthless!"
Then he goes out and brags,
"Look at the great bargain I got!"

¹⁵You may have an abundance of wealth,
Piles of gold and jewels,
But there is something of far greater worth—
Speaking revelation-words of knowledge.

---

a. 20:9 The Hebrew word for "clean" can also be translated, "perfect" or "holy." The word for "pure" can also be translated, "clear, bright, shining, unmixed." Yet, through God's grace, by the blood of Jesus, believers have been purified, made holy, and set free from our sins.
b. 20:13 The Septuagint reads, "Don't love speaking evil."

¹⁶Anyone stupid enough to guarantee a loan for a stranger^a
Deserves to have his property held as security.

¹⁷What you obtain dishonestly may seem sweet at first,
But sooner or later, you'll live to regret it!^b

¹⁸If you solicit good advice, then your plans will succeed!
So don't charge into battle without wisdom,
For wars are won by skillful strategy.

¹⁹A blabbermouth will reveal your secrets, so stay away
From people who can't keep their mouths shut.^c

²⁰If you despise your father or mother,
Your life will flicker out like a lamp
Extinguished into the deepest darkness.
²¹If an inheritance is gained too early in life,
It will not be blessed in the end.

²²Don't ever say, "I'm going to get even with them
If it's the last thing I do!"
Wrap God's grace around your heart,
And He will be the One to vindicate you!"

²³The Lord hates double standards;
That's hypocrisy at its worst!^d

²⁴It is the Lord who directs your life,
For each step you take is ordained by God
To bring you closer to your destiny—
So much of your life, then, remains a mystery!^e

²⁵Be careful in making a rash promise before God,
Or you may be trapped by your vow
And live to regret it!

---

a. 20:16 Some manuscripts have, "a promiscuous woman."
b. 20:17 Or, "The bread of falsehood may taste sweet at first, but afterwards you'll have a mouth full of gravel."
c. 20:19 The Aramaic adds a line, "One who is faithful in spirit hides a matter."
d. 20:23 Or, "The Lord hates differing weights and dishonest scales are wicked."
e. 20:24 The Aramaic reads, "So what man is capable of ordering his way?"

[26]A wise king is able to discern corruption
And remove wickedness from his kingdom.[a]

[27]The spirit God breathed into man,[b]
Is like a living lamp and shining light—
Searching into the innermost chamber of our being!

[28]Good leadership[c] is built upon love and truth,
For kindness and integrity is what keeps leaders
In their position of trust.

[29]We admire the young for their strength and beauty,
But the dignity of the old is their wisdom.[d]

[30]When you are punished severely,
You learn your lesson well—
For your painful experience does wonders
To change your life.

Chapter 21

God is the Source of Wisdom

[1]It's as easy for God to steer a king's heart[e]
For His purposes,
As it is for Him to direct the course of a stream.[f]

[2]You may think you're right all the time,
But God thoroughly examines our motives.

---

a. 20:26 Or, "A wise king winnows the wicked and turns his chariot wheel over them."
b. 20:27 Implied by the Hebrew word, *nishmat,* used in Genesis 2:7.
c. 20:28 Or, "A king's throne."
d. 20:29 Or, "their grey hair."
e. 21:1 Don't forget, we have been made kings and priests by the blood of the Lamb. See 1 Peter 2:9; Revelation 1:6; and 5:10.
f. 21:1 Because a leader's decisions affect so many people, God will intervene and steer them, as a farmer steers the course of a stream to irrigate his fields.

Proverbs 21

³It pleases God more when we
Demonstrate godliness and justice,
Than to merely offer Him a sacrifice.

⁴Arrogance, superiority, and pride
Are the fruits of wickedness,ᵃ
And the true definition of sin!

⁵Brilliant ideas pay off and bring you prosperity,
But making hasty, impatient decisions
Will only lead to financial loss.ᵇ
⁶You can make a fortune dishonestly,
But your crime will hold you
In the snares of death!ᶜ
⁷Violent rebels don't have a chance,
For their rejection of truth and
Their love of evil will drag them
Deeper into darkness.
⁸You can discern that a person is guilty
By their devious actions,
And the innocence of a person
By their honest, sincere ways.

⁹It's better to live all alone in a rickety shack
Than to share a castle with a crabby spouse!ᵈ

¹⁰The wicked always craves what is evil;
They'll show no mercy and get no mercy.ᵉ

¹¹Senseless people learn their lessons the hard way,
But the wise are teachable.
¹²A godly, righteous personᶠ has the ability

---

a. 21:4 Or, "the tillage of the wicked." The Aramaic and the Septuagint has, "the lamp of the wicked."
b. 21:5 The Aramaic is, "The thoughts of the chosen one are trusting, but those of the evil one lead to poverty." This verse is missing from the Septuagint.
c. 21:6 As translated from the Aramaic and the Septuagint. The Hebrew is, "the money will vanish into thin air."
d. 21:9 The Septuagint reads, "It's better to live in the corner of an attic than a large home plastered with unrighteousness."
e. 21:10 The Hebrew is, "They show no mercy," while the Septuagint reads, "They'll receive no mercy." The translator has chosen to merge both concepts.
f. 21:12 The Hebrew is, "a righteous one," which can also speak of God, "the Righteous One."

To bring the light of instruction to the wicked,
Even though they despise what the wicked do.[a]

[13]If you close your heart to the cries of the poor,
Then I'll close My ears when you cry out to Me!

[14]Try giving a secret gift
To the one who is angry with you,
And watch his anger disappear.
A kind generous gift goes a long way
To soothe the anger of one who is livid.[b]

[15]When justice is served,
The lovers of God celebrate and rejoice,
But the wicked begin to panic.
[16]When you forsake the ways of wisdom,
You will wander into the realm of dark spirits.[c]
[17]To love pleasure for pleasure's sake
Will introduce you to poverty.
Indulging in a life of sybaritic luxury[d]
Will never make you wealthy!
[18]The wicked bring on themselves
The very suffering they planned for others,
For their treachery comes back to haunt them.[e]

[19]It's better to live in a hut in the wilderness
Than with a crabby, scolding spouse!

[20]In wisdom's house, you'll find delightful treasures
And the oil of the Holy Spirit[f]
But the stupid[g] squander what they've been given.
[21]The lovers of God who chase after righteousness

---

a. 21:12 As translated from the Septuagint. There are many examples of this in the Bible: Daniel in Babylon, Joseph in Egypt, and the follower of Jesus today, living among unbelievers.
b. 21:14 The Aramaic and Septuagint translate this: "He that withholds a gift arouses anger."
c. 21:16 Or, "the congregation of the Rephaim." The Rephaim were a pagan tribe of giants and are now equated with spirits of darkness. See Genesis 14:5 and Deuteronomy 2:11.
d. 21:17 Or, "the lover of wine and oil."
e. 21:18 Or, "The evil become the ransom payment for the righteous, and the faithless for the upright."
f. 21:20 The Hebrew is, "oil," an emblem of the Holy Spirit.
g. 21:20 Or, "a fool of a man."

Will find all their dreams come true:
An abundant life drenched with favor,
And a fountain that overflows with satisfaction.[a]

[22]A warrior filled with wisdom
Ascends into the high place
And releases regional breakthrough,
Bringing down the strongholds of the mighty.[b]

[23]Watch your words and be careful what you say,
And you'll be surprised
How few troubles you'll have!
[24]An arrogant man is inflated with pride,
Nothing but a snooty scoffer
In love with his own opinion—
"Mr. Mocker" is his name![c]
[25-26]Taking the easy way out is the habit of a lazy man
And it will be his downfall!
All day long he thinks about
All the things that he craves,
For he hasn't learned the secret
That the generous man has learned:
Extravagant giving never leads to poverty.[d]
[27]To bring an offering to God
With an ulterior motive is detestable,
For it amounts to nothing but hypocrisy!

[28]No one believes a notorious liar,
But the guarded words of an honest man
Stand the test of time.

[29]The wicked are shameless and stubborn,
But the lovers of God have a holy confidence.

[30]All your brilliant wisdom and clever insight
Will be of no help at all

---

a. 21:21 Or "righteousness."

b. 21:22 Or, "demolishing their strength of confidence."

c. 21:24 The Septuagint adds a line, "He who holds a grudge is a sinner."

d. 21:25-26 This is implied in the context and is necessary to complete the meaning of the proverb. The last line of this verse reads in the Septuagint: "the righteous lavish on others mercy and compassion."

If the Lord is against you.
[31]You can do your best to prepare for the battle[a]
But ultimate victory comes from the Lord God.

Chapter 22

How to Live a Life of Wisdom

[1]A beautiful reputation[b] is more to be desired
Than great riches,
And to be lovingly esteemed by others
Is more honorable than to own immense investments.[c]

[2]The rich and the poor
Have one thing in common:
The Lord God created each one.

[3]A prudent person with insight foresees
Danger coming and prepares himself for it,[d]
But the senseless rush blindly forward
And suffer the consequences!
[4]Laying your life down
In tender surrender before the Lord
Will bring life, prosperity, and honor as your reward.

[5]Twisted and perverse lives
Are surrounded by demonic influence.[e]
If you value your soul, stay far away from them.

[6]Dedicate your children to God
And point them in the way that they should go;[f]

---

a. 21:31 Or, "the horse is prepared for the battle."
b. 22:1 The Hebrew is simply, "Name preferred to wealth." The Aramaic indicates it could be "The Name [of God]."
c. 22:1 Or, "silver and gold." Remember, it is Solomon, one of the richest men to ever live who penned these words.
d. 22:3 Wise people solve problems before they happen.
e. 22:5 Or, "thorns and snares." This becomes a metaphor of demonic curses and troubles. Thorns are associated with the fall of Adam (Jesus wore a crown of *thorns* and took away our *curse*). The "snares" picture the temptations of evil that the Devil places in our path.
f. 22:6 Or, "Train them in the direction they are best suited to go." Some Jewish scholars teach that this means understanding your children's talents and then seeing that they go into that field.

And the values they've learned from you
Will be with them for life.

[7]If you borrow money with interest,
You'll end up serving the interests of your creditors,[a]
For the rich rule over the poor.
[8]Sin is a seed that brings a harvest;
You'll reap a heap of trouble
With every seed you plant,
For your investment in sin pays a full return—
The full punishment you deserve![b]
[9]When you are generous[c] to the poor you are
Enriched with blessings in return.

[10]Say good-bye to a troublemaker,
And you'll say goodbye to
Quarrels, strife, tension, and arguments,
For a troublemaker traffics in shame.[d]

[11]The Lord loves those whose hearts are holy
And He is the Friend of those whose ways are pure.[e]
[12]God passionately watches[f] over
His deep well[g] of revelation-knowledge,
But He subverts the lies of those who pervert the truth.
[13]A slacker always has an excuse
For not working—
Like, "I can't go to work! There's a lion outside
And murderers too!"[h]
[14]Sex with an adulteress

---

a. 22:7 The Septuagint reads, "The servant will lend to his own master."
b. 22:8 As translated from the Septuagint.
c. 22:9 The Hebrew word for "generous" is actually, "to have a bountiful eye." It is a figure of speech for generosity, a life of helping others.
d. 22:10 As translated from the Aramaic.
e. 22:11 As translated from the Septuagint. For the follower of Jesus, we enjoy a relationship with our holy King as we live in the light and love to please Him.
f. 22:12 Or, "the eyes of the Lord." In the church today, prophets become "eyes" in the body of Christ. They see and reveal God's heart for His people.
g. 22:12 Although the concept of a well is not found in the Hebrew; it is added by the translator for poetic nuance.
h. 22:13 This humorous verse uses both satire and a metaphor. There's always an excuse for not working hard. The Aramaic text adds, "and a murderer too!"

Is like falling into the abyss,
Those under God's curse jump right in
To their own destruction.
[15]Although rebellion is woven into a young man's heart,[a]
Tough discipline can make him into a man.
[16]There are two kinds of people
Headed toward poverty:
Those who exploit the poor
And those who bribe the rich.[b]

Sayings of the Wise

[17]Listen carefully and open your heart;[c]
Drink in the wise revelation that I impart.
[18]When you treasure the beauty of my words,
You'll become winsome and wise.
Always be prepared to share my words
At the appropriate time.
[19]For I'm releasing these words to you this day;
Yes, even to you, so that your living hope
Will be found in God alone,
For He's the only one who is always true!
[20-21]Pay attention to these
Excellent sayings of threefold things.[d]
From within my words you will discover
True and reliable revelation.
They will give you serenity,[e] so that you can reveal
The truth of the word of the One who sends you.

---

a. 22:15 The Aramaic word used here means, "senseless."

b. 22:16 The Hebrew is literally, "Oppressing the poor is gain, giving to the rich is loss—both end up only in poverty."

c. From this verse to 24:22 we have a collection of proverbs that focus on virtue. They are especially designed for the young person about to enter a career and start a family.

d. 22:20-21 As translated from the Aramaic. Most translators find this verse difficult to convey. The Hebrew can be, "I have written excellent things," "I have written three times," "I write thirty sayings," "I have written you previously," or "I have written you, officers." The Septuagint reads, "You should copy these things three times." If the Proverbs contain keys to understanding riddles and mysteries (Proverbs 1:2-6), then we have one of those keys given to us here. God speaks in *threes*—for He is a triune God. We have a body, soul, and spirit. God lived in a three room house (outer court, Holy Place, and the chamber of the Holy of Holies). These threefold dimensions are throughout the Bible.

e. 22:20-21 "Serenity" is only found in the Aramaic.

Proverbs 22

²²Never oppress the poor
Or pass laws with the motive of crushing the weak.
²³For the Lord will rise to plead their case
And humiliate the one who humiliates the poor.^a

^{24–25}Walk away from an angry man
Or you'll embrace a snare in your soul^b
By becoming bad-tempered just like him.

²⁶Why would you ever guarantee a loan for someone else
Or promise to be responsible for their debts?
²⁷For if you fail to pay, you could lose your shirt!^c

²⁸The previous generation has set boundaries in place;
Don't you dare move them just to benefit yourself.^d

²⁹If you are uniquely gifted in your work
You will rise and be promoted;
You won't be held back—
You'll stand before kings!

Chapter 23

Wisdom Will Protect You

¹If you've been invited to dine
With a very important person,
Consider your manners and
Keep in mind who you're with;
²Be careful to curb your appetite.
³Don't be deceived by all his delicacies
For they may have another motive
In having you sit at their table.

---

a. 22:23 As translated from the Aramaic. The Hebrew is, "He will rob the soul of the one who robs the poor."
b. 22:24-25 As translated from the Aramaic.
c. 22:27 Or "bed."
d. 22:28 This refers to either moving the property lines of your neighbors to take more land, or it could refer to moving landmarks and memorials placed there by our ancestors. Yet it also speaks to the moral boundaries that the previous generation modeled for us; they are to be upheld.

[4]Don't compare yourself to the rich[a];
Surrender your selfish ambition,
And evaluate them properly.
[5]For no sooner do you start counting your wealth
That it sprouts wings and flies away
Like an eagle in the sky—
Here today, gone tomorrow!
[6]Be sensible when you dine with a stingy man[b]
And don't eat more than you should[c]
[7]For he's a tightwad
Who only has one thing on his mind:
"How much is this going to cost me?"
He will grudgingly say, "Go ahead and eat all you want,"
But in his heart he resents the fact
That he has to pay for your meal.
[8]You'll be sorry you ate anything at all[d]
And all your compliments will be wasted.

[9]A rebellious fool will despise your wise advice,
So don't even waste your time—save your breath!

[10]Never move a long-standing boundary line
Or attempt to take land
That belongs to the fatherless.
[11]For they have a mighty Protector,
A loving Redeemer,[e] who watches over them
And He will stand up for their cause.

[12]Pay close attention
To the teaching that corrects you,
And open your heart
To every word of instruction.

---

a. 23:4 As translated from the Septuagint.
b. 23:6 The Hebrew is literally, "an evil eye," which is a metaphor for a stingy man.
c. 23:6 Or, "Don't crave his delicacies."
d. 23:8 Or, "You'll vomit up the little you've eaten."
e. 23:11 The Hebrew word is *goel*, which means "Kinsman-Redeemer." The Aramaic word means "Savior." This shows powerfully how God will take up the grievances of the oppressed.

[13]Don't withhold appropriate discipline from your child;
Go ahead and punish him when he needs it;[a]
Don't worry—it won't kill him!
[14]A good spanking could be the very thing
That teaches him a lifelong lesson![b]
[15]My beloved child,
When your heart is full of wisdom,
My heart is full of gladness.
[16]And when you speak anointed words,[c]
We are speaking mouth to mouth![d]
[17]Don't allow the actions of evil men
To cause you to burn with anger.[e]
Instead, burn with unrelenting passion
As you worship God in holy awe.
[18]Your future is bright and filled with
A living hope that will never fade away.

[19]As you listen to me, my beloved child,
You will grow in wisdom
And your heart will be drawn into
Understanding to make right decisions.[f]

[20]Don't live in the excesses of drunkenness
Or gluttony, or wasting your life away
By partying all the time.[g]
[21]Because drunkards and gluttons
Sleep their lives away and end up broke!

---

a. 23:13 The Hebrew is, "strike them with the rod."
b. 23:14 Or, "rescues him from death." The Hebrew word is Sheol."
c. 23:16 Or, "speak what is right."
d. 23:16 This is taken from the Septuagint, which is literally, "your lips shall speak with my lips." The Hebrew is, "my kidneys (soul) will rejoice." See Numbers 12:6-8 which reveals that God spoke with Moses, *mouth to mouth* (Literal Hebrew).
e. 23:17 The Hebrew word used here describes an emotion of intense passion. Many translate it "envy," ("do not envy the sinner) but that does not describe it fully. Another possible translation would be "zeal."
f. 23:19 The Aramaic is, "Set up my doctrines in your heart."
g. 23:20 Translated from the Aramaic and the Septuagint.

²²Give respect to your father and mother,
For without them you wouldn't even be here,
And don't neglect them when they grow old.

²³Embrace the truthª and hold it close.
Don't let go of wisdom, instruction,
And life-giving understanding.

²⁴When a father observes his child living in godliness,
He is ecstatic with joy—nothing makes him prouder!
²⁵So may your father's heart burst with joy,
And your mother's soul be filled with gladness—
All because of you!

²⁶My son, give me your heart
And embrace fully what I'm about to tell you:
²⁷Stay far away from prostitutes
And you'll stay far away
From the pit of destruction.
For sleeping with a promiscuous woman
Is like falling into a trap
That you'll never be able to escape!
²⁸Like a robber hiding in the shadows,
She's waiting to claim another victim—
Another husband unfaithful to his wife.

²⁹Who has anguish? Who has bitter sorrow?
Who constantly complains and argues?
Who stumbles and falls and hurts himself?
Who's the one with bloodshot eyes?
³⁰It's the one who drinks too much,
And is always looking for a brew;
Make sure it's never you!
³¹And don't be drunk with wineᵇ
But be known as one who enjoys

---

a. 23:23 The Hebrew word is literally, "create the truth" or "give birth to truth," or, "possess the truth." This Hebrew word is also used for God as the Creator. See Genesis 14:19, 22.
b. 23:31 As translated from the Septuagint.

Proverbs 23

The company of the lovers of God,[a]
32For drunkenness brings the sting of a serpent,
Like the fangs of a viper upon your soul.
33It will make you hallucinate, mumble,
And speak words that are perverse.
34You'll be like a seasick sailor,
Being tossed to and fro,
Dizzy and out of your mind.
35You'll awake only to say, "What hit me?
I feel like I've been run over by a truck!"
Yet off you'll go, looking for another drink!

Chapter 24

Wisdom's Warning

1Don't envy the wealth of the wicked
Or crave their company.
2For they're obsessed with causing trouble
And their conversations are corrupt.

3Wise people are builders[b]—
They build families, businesses, communities,
And through intelligence and insight,
Their enterprises are established and endure.
4Because of their skilled leadership,
The hearts[c] of people are filled with
The treasures of wisdom and
The pleasures of spiritual wealth.

---

a. 23:31 As translated from the Septuagint and a marginal reading of the Hebrew. The Aramaic is, "Meditate on righteousness." The Septuagint adds a line not found in Hebrew or Aramaic that describes the unflattering life of a drunk: "You will walk around naked as a pestle!"
b. 24:3 Or, "A house is built by wisdom." The "house" is more than a structure with a roof and a floor. It becomes a metaphor of families, churches, businesses, and enterprises.
c. 24:4 Or, "inner chambers."

⁵Wisdom can make anyone into a mighty warrior,[a]
And revelation-knowledge increases strength.
⁶Wise strategy is necessary to wage war,
And with many astute advisers,
You'll see the path to victory more clearly.

⁷Wisdom is a treasure too lofty[b]
For a quarreling fool—
He'll have nothing to say
When leaders gather together.

⁸There is one who makes plans to do evil,
"Master Schemer" is his name.

⁹If you plan to do evil, it's as wrong as doing it,
And everyone detests a troublemaker.

¹⁰If you faint under pressure,
You have no courage![c]

¹¹Go and rescue the perishing! Be their savior!
Why would you stand back and watch them
Stagger to their death?
¹²And why would you say, "But it's none of my business?"
Yet the One who knows you completely
And judges your every motive
Is also the keeper of souls—not just yours!
And He sees through your excuses
And holds you responsible
For failing to help those whose lives are threatened!

¹³Revelation-knowledge is a delicacy,
Sweet like flowing honey that melts in your mouth,

---

a. 24:5 Or, "Wisdom makes anyone into a hero." The Aramaic and the Septuagint reads, "It's better to be wise than to be strong."

b. 24:7 The Hebrew is actually, "Wisdom is coral to a fool." That is, it is unattainable, deep, and hidden.

c. 24:10 Or, "your strength is limited." Our weakness always becomes an excuse to quit, but strength and courage come as the result of faithfulness under pressure. Some interpret this to mean, "If you fail to help others in their time of need you will grow too weak to help yourself."

Eat as much of it as you can, my friend!
[14]For then you will perceive what is true wisdom;
Your future will be bright,[a]
And this hope living within,
Will never disappoint you!

[15]Listen up, you irreverent ones—
Don't harass the lovers of God[b]
And don't invade their resting place.
[16]For the lovers of God may suffer adversity
And stumble seven times,
But they will continue to rise
Over and over again!
But the unrighteous are
Brought down by just one calamity
And will never be able to rise again.[c]

[17]Never gloat when your enemy meets disaster
And don't be quick to rejoice if he falls,
[18]For the Lord who sees your heart
Will be displeased with you,
And will pity your foe.

[19]Don't be angrily offended over evildoers
Or be agitated by them,[d]
[20]For the wicked have no life and no future—
Their light of life will die out.[e]

[21]My child, stand in awe of the Lord Jehovah!
Give counsel to others,
But don't mingle with those who are rebellious.
[22]For sudden destruction will fall upon them
And their lives will be ruined in a moment
And who knows what retribution they will face![f]

---

a. 24:14 The Septuagint is, "Your death will be good."
b. 24:15 Or, "the righteous."
c. 24:16 Implied in the text as it completes the parallelism.
d. 24:19 The Septuagint is, "Don't rejoice with those who do evil or be jealous of them."
e. 24:20 Not only will they "die out", but the implication is that they will have no posterity.
f. 24:22 Verses 21 & 22 are translated from the Aramaic.

Revelation from the Wise

[23]Those enlightened with wisdom
Have spoken these proverbs:

Judgment must be impartial.
For it is always wrong to be swayed by a person's status.
[24]If you say to the guilty, "You are innocent,"
The nation will curse you
And the people will revile you.
[25]But when you convict the guilty,
The people will thank you
And reward you with favor.

[26]Speaking honestly is a
Sign of true friendship.[a]

[27]Go ahead, build your career
And give yourself to your work,
But if you put Me first,
You'll see your family be built up![b]

[28]Why would you be a false accuser,
And slander with your words?
[29]Don't ever spitefully say, "I'll get even with him!
I'll do to him what he did to me!"

[30-31]One day I passed by the field of a lazy man,
And I noticed the vineyards of a slacker.
I observed nothing but thorns, weeds,
And broken down walls.
[32]So I considered their lack of wisdom,
And I pondered the lessons
I could learn from this:
[33-34] "Professional work habits
Prevent poverty from becoming your

---

a. 24:26 The Hebrew is literally, "An honest answer is like a kiss on the lips." In the culture of the day, kissing was a sign of authentic friendship and a mark of relationship which was often expressed in public among friends.
b. 24:27 As translated from the Septuagint.

Permanent business partner!"
And,
"If you put off until tomorrow the work
You could do today,
Tomorrow never seems to come."

Chapter 25

[1]Solomon's Proverbs Published by
The Scribes of King Hezekiah

[2]God conceals the revelation of His Word[a]
In the hiding place of His glory.[b]
But the honor of kings[c] is revealed to all
By how they thoroughly mine out
The deeper meaning of all that God says.
[3]The heart of a king is full of understanding
Like the heavens are high and the ocean is deep.
[4]If you burn away the impurities from silver,
A sterling vessel will emerge from the fire;
[5]And if you purge corruption from the kingdom,
A king's reign will be established in righteousness.
[6]Don't boast in the presence of a king
Or promote yourself by taking a seat at the head table,
And pretend that you're someone important.
[7]For it is better for the king to say to you,
"Come, you should sit at the head table,"
Than for him to say in front of everyone,
"Please get up and move;
You're sitting in the place of the prince."

[8]Don't be hasty to file a lawsuit,
Starting something you wish you hadn't;
You could be humiliated when you lose your case!

---

a. 25:2 Many translate this "a matter," whereas the Hebrew is *dabar*, which is translated over eight hundred times in the Old Testament as "word."
b. 25:2 There is beautiful poetry in the Hebrew text. The word for "hide" is *cathar* and the word for "word" is *dabar*. The Hebrew is actually, *kabod* (glory) *cathar* (hidden) *dabar* (word).
c. 25:2 We have been made kings and priests, royal lovers of God because of God's grace and Christ's redeeming blood. See 1 Peter 2:9 and Revelation 5:8-10.

[9]Don't reveal another person's secret
Just to prove a point in an argument.
Or you could be accused of being a gossip,
[10]And gain a reputation of being one
Who betrays the confidence of a friend.
[11]Winsome words spoken
At just the right time[a]
Are as appealing as apples gilded in gold
And surrounded with silver.[b]

[12]To humbly receive wise correction
Adorns your life with beauty[c]
And makes you a better person.

[13]A reliable, trustworthy messenger
Refreshes the heart of his master,[d]
Like a gentle breeze blowing at harvest time—
Cooling the sweat off of his brow.

[14]Clouds that carry no water,
And a wind that brings no refreshing rain[e]—
That's what you're like
When you boast of a gift that you don't have.[f]

Wisdom Practices Self-Control
[15]Use patience and kindness when you
Want to persuade a leader,

---

a. 25:11 The Aramaic reads, "The one who speaks the Word is an apple of gold in a setting of silver." The Septuagint is, "A wise word is like a golden apple in a pendant of rubies."
b. 25:11 Each one of God's promises are like "apples gilded in gold." When we are full of His Spirit, we can speak and prophesy words of encouragement that are spoken at the right time for the blessing of others.
c. 25:12 Or, "an earring of gold, an ornament of fine gold." The earring pierces our ear and is an emblem of a listening heart.
d. 25:13 Or "employer."
e. 25:14 The symbols of clouds, wind, and rain are significant. Clouds are often a metaphor for the people of God filled with glory (Hebrews 12:1; Revelation 1:7). Wind is an emblem of the Holy Spirit bringing new life (John 3:6-8) and rain often points to teaching the revelation truths that refresh and water the seeds of spiritual growth (Isaiah 55:8-11). God's anointed people are to be clouds carried by the wind of the Holy Spirit, that bring refreshing truths to His people. When we are empty and false, we are clouds without rain. See 2 Peter 2:17 and Jude 12.
f. 25:14 Or, "boast of a promised gift you never intend to give." The Hebrew is literally, "to make yourself shine in a gift of falsehood."

And watch them change their mind
Right in front of you;
For your gentle wisdom
Will quell the strongest resistance.[a]

[16]When you discover something sweet,
Don't overindulge and eat more than you need,
For excess in anything can make you
Sick of even a good thing.

[17]Don't wear out your welcome by staying too long
At the home of your friends, or they may get fed up with
Always having you there and wish you wouldn't come!

[18]Lying about, and slandering someone
Is as bad as hitting them with a club,
Or wounding them with an arrow,
Or stabbing them with a sword.

[19]You can't depend upon an unreliable person
When you really need help!
It can be compared to biting down
On an abscessed tooth
Or walking with a sprained ankle!

[20]When you sing a song of joy to someone suffering
In the deepest grief and heartache,
It can be compared to stealing their coat
In the middle of a blizzard,
Or rubbing salt in their wound.

[21]Is your enemy hungry? Buy him lunch.
Win him over with your kindness.[b]
[22]Your surprising generosity
Will awaken his conscience,[c]
And God will reward you with favor.
[23]As the north wind brings a storm,

---

a. 25:15 Or, "Soft words break bones."
b. 25:21 Or, "Is he thirsty? Give him a drink."
c. 25:22 Or, "You will heap coals of fire on his head." His heart will be moved and his shame exposed.

Saying things you shouldn't[a]
Brings a storm to any relationship.

[24]It's better to live all alone in a rundown shack
Than to share a castle with a crabby spouse![b]

[25]Like a drink of cool water to a weary, thirsty soul—
So hearing good news revives the spirit.[c]

[26]When a lover of God gives in
And compromises with wickedness,
It can be compared to contaminating
A stream with sewage or polluting a fountain.

[27]It's good to eat sweet things,
But you can take too much.
It's good to be honored,
But to seek words of praise[d]
Is not honor at all!

[28]If you live without restraint,
And are unable to control your temper,
You're as helpless as a city
With broken-down defenses, open to attack.

Chapter 26

Don't Be a Fool

[1]It is totally out of place
To promote and honor a fool,
Just like it's out of place to have
Snow in the summer
And rain at harvest time.[e]

---

a. 25:23 Or, "words of gossip."
b. 25:24 With the exception of one Hebrew letter, this verse is identical to 21:9. See footnote. The Aramaic reads, "than to live with a contentious woman in a house of divisions."
c. 25:25 Implied in the text.
d. 25:27 This line is translated from the Aramaic.
e. 26:1 Both snow and rain are good in their proper season but harmful in the wrong season. In the same way, it is harmful to the fool if you affirm him and honor him prematurely.

[2]An undeserved curse will be
Powerless to harm you;
It may flutter over you like a bird
But it will find no place to land.[a]

[3]Guide a horse with a whip,
Direct a donkey with a bridle,
And a rebellious fool
With a beating on his backside!

[4]Don't respond to the words of a fool
With more foolish words,
Or you will become as foolish as he is!
[5]Yet, if you're asked a silly question,
Answer it with words of wisdom[b]
So the fool doesn't think he's so clever.

[6]If you chose a fool to represent you
You're asking for trouble;
It will be as bad for you
As cutting off your own feet!

[7]You can never trust the words of a fool
Just like a crippled man can't trust
His legs to support him.[c]

[8]Give honor to a fool
And watch it backfire—
Like a stone tied to a slingshot!

[9]The statements of a fool will hurt others[d]
Like a thorn bush brandished by a drunk.

[10]Like a reckless archer shooting arrows at random
Is the impatient employer who hires

---

a. 26:2 There is an implication in some Hebrew manuscripts that the "curse" will go back
and land on the one who wrongly spoke it, like a bird going back to its nest.
b. 26:5 As translated from the Aramaic.
c. 26:7 As translated from the Aramaic.
d. 26:9 As translated from the Aramaic.

Just any fool who comes along—
Someone's going to get hurt!^a

¹¹Fools are famous for repeating their errors
Like dogs are known to return to their vomit.

¹²There's only one thing worse than a fool,
And that's the smug, conceited man
Always in love with his own opinions!

Don't Be Lazy

¹³The lazy loafer says:
"I can't go out and look for a job—
There may be a lion out there
Roaming wild in the streets!"

¹⁴As a door is hinged to the wall,
So the lazy man keeps turning over,
Hinged to his bed!
¹⁵There are some people so lazy,
They won't even work to feed themselves!

¹⁶A self-righteous person^b
Is convinced he's smarter
Than seven wise counselors
Who tell him the truth.

¹⁷It's better to grab a mad dog by its ears
Than to meddle and interfere in a quarrel^c
That's none of your business.

Watch Your Words

¹⁸⁻¹⁹The one who is caught lying to his friend
And says, "I didn't mean it; I was only joking,"
Can be compared to a madman

---

a. 26:10 Implied in the context. This is a very difficult verse to translate and reads quite differently in the Aramaic and the Septuagint. The Aramaic is, "A fool suffers much like a drunkard crossing the sea." And the Septuagint reads, "Every fool endures much hardship and their fury comes to nothing."
b. 26:16 Or "sluggard." This speaks of a person who lives in fantasy and not reality.
c. 26:17 Or, "to become furious because of a quarrel that's not yours."

Randomly shooting off deadly weapons!
[20]It takes fuel to have a fire—
A fire dies down when you run out of fuel,
So quarrels disappear when the gossip ends.
[21]Add fuel to the fire and the blaze goes on;
Add an argumentative man to the mix
And you'll keep strife alive.
[22]Gossip is so delicious,
And how we love to swallow it,
For slander[a] is easily absorbed
Into our innermost being!

[23]Smooth talk[b] can hide a corrupt heart
Just like a pretty glaze covers a cheap clay pot.
[24]Kind words can be a cover
To conceal hatred of others,
For hypocrisy loves to hide behind flattery.
[25]So don't be drawn in by the hypocrite,
For his gracious speech is a charade,
Nothing but a masquerade,
Covering his hatred and evil on parade.[c]
[26]Don't worry; he can't keep the mask on for long.
One day his hypocrisy will be exposed
Before all the world!

[27]Go ahead, set a trap for others—
And then watch as it snaps back upon you!
Start a landslide and you'll be the one
Who gets crushed!

[28]Hatred is the root of slander,[d]
And insecurity the root of flattery.[e]

---

a. 26:22 Or "complaining."
b. 26:23 As translated from the Septuagint. The Hebrew is, "Burning words."
c. 26:25 The Hebrew is, "seven abominations hide in his heart." This is a figure of speech for the fullness of evil, a heart filled to the brim with darkness.
d. 26:28 Or, "A slanderer hates his victims."
e. 26:28 Implied in the text. The Aramaic is, "malicious words work trouble."

Chapter 27

Heed Wisdom's Warnings

¹Never brag about the plans you have for tomorrow
For you don't have a clue
What tomorrow may bring to you!

²Let someone else honor you
For your accomplishments,
For self-praise is never appropriate.

³It's easier to carry a heavy boulder and a ton of sand
Than to be provoked by a fool
And have to carry that burden!

⁴The rage and anger of others can be overwhelming,
But it's nothing compared to jealousy's fire!

⁵It's better to be corrected openly,
If it stems from hidden love.
⁶You can trust a friend who
Wounds you with his honesty,[a]
But your enemy's pretended flattery[b]
Comes from insincerity.

⁷When your soul is full, you turn down
Even the sweetest honey;
But when your soul is starving,
Every bitter thing becomes sweet.[c]

⁸Like a bird that has fallen from its nest
Is the one who is dislodged from his home.[d]

⁹Sweet friendships[e] refresh the soul,
And awaken our hearts with joy,

---

a. 27:6 Or, "Wounds by a loved one are long lasting (effective and faithful)."
b. 27:6 Or "kisses."
c. 27:7 When we are full of many things and many opinions, the sweet Word of God, like revelation-honey, is spurned. Instead, we eat and fill our souls with things that never satisfy.
d. 27:8 Or, "banished from his place." As translated from the Aramaic.
e. 27:9 Or "counsel."

For good friends are like the anointing oil
That yields the fragrant incense of God's presence.[a]
[10]So never give up on a friend,
Or abandon a friend of your father—
For in the day of your brokenness[b]
You won't have to run to a relative for help,
For a friend nearby
Is better than a relative far away.

[11]My son, when you walk in wisdom,
My heart is filled with gladness,
For the way you live is proof
That I've not taught you in vain.[c]

[12]A wise, shrewd person
Discerns the danger ahead
And prepares himself,
But the naïve simpleton never looks ahead
And suffers the consequences.

[13]Cosign for one you barely know
And you will pay a great price!
Anyone stupid enough to guarantee
The loan of another deserves to have
His property seized in payment.

[14]Do you think you're blessing your neighbors
When you sing at the top of your lungs
Early in the morning?
Don't be fooled—
They'll curse you for doing it![d]
[15]An endless drip, drip, drip, from a leaky faucet[e]
And the words of a cranky, nagging wife
Have the same effect.

---

a. 27:9 Implied in the text. The Hebrew text refers to the sacred "anointing oil" and the "incense" that burns in the Holy Place.
b. 27:10 As translated from the Aramaic.
c. 27:11 Implied in the text.
d. 27:14 Or, "He that sings in a loud voice early in the morning, thinking he's blessing his neighbor is no different than he that pronounces a curse."
e. 27:15 Or, "A constant drip on a rainy day."

[16]Can you stop the north wind from blowing
Or grasp a handful of oil?
That's easier to do than to stop her from complaining.

[17]It takes a grinding wheel to sharpen a blade,
And so a friendly argument can sharpen a man.[a]

[18]Tend an orchard and you'll have fruit to eat;
Serve the master's interests
And you'll receive honor that's sweet.

[19]Just as no two faces are alike,
So every heart is different.[b]

[20]Hell and destruction are never filled,
And so the desires of men's hearts
Are insatiable.

[21]Fire is the way to test the purity of silver and gold,
But the character of a man is tested
By giving him a measure of fame.[c]

[22]You can beat a fool half to death,
And still never beat the foolishness out of him.[d]

[23]A shepherd[e] should pay close attention
To the faces of his flock,
And hold close to his heart the condition
Of those he cares for.

[24]A man's strength, power, and riches[f]
Will one day fade away;
Not even nations[g] endure forever.
[25-27]Take care of your responsibilities

---

a. 27:17 Or, "a man's face."
b. 27:19 As translated from the Aramaic and the Septuagint.
c. 27:21 Or, "By the things he praises."
d. 27:22 Or, "If you pound a fool in a mortar, like dried grain with a pestle, still his foolishness would not depart from him."
e. 27:23 Implied in the text.
f. 27:24 The Hebrew is only, "riches," while the Aramaic adds, "power (dominion)" and the Septuagint adds, "strength." The translator has chosen to combine them.
g. 27:24 Or, "a crown (dominion)."

And be diligent in your business
And you will have more than enough—
An abundance of food, clothing,
And plenty for your household.[a]

Chapter 28

Lovers of God

[1]Guilty criminals experience paranoia
Even though no one threatens them,
But the innocent lovers of God,
Because of righteousness, will
Have the boldness[b] of a young, ferocious lion!

[2]A rebellious nation is thrown into chaos[c]
But leaders anointed with wisdom
Will restore law and order.

[3]When a pauper[d] oppresses the destitute,
It's like a flash flood
That sweeps away their last hope.

[4]Those who turn their backs
On what they know is right,[e]
Will no longer be able to tell right from wrong,
But those who love the truth
Strengthen their souls.[f]

[5]Justice never makes sense to men
Devoted to darkness,

---

a. 27:25-27 An agricultural analogy is used in the Hebrew and Aramaic. The analogy of a farming enterprise has been changed to "business" in order to transfer meaning. It is literally, "Gather the hay of the field and hills, and new grass will appear. Lambs will provide clothing, goats will pay for the price of the field, and there will be enough goat's milk for you, your family, and your servant girls."
b. 28:1 Or "confidence."
c. 28:2 Or, "A rebellious nation will have one leader after another."
d. 28:3 This "pauper" can also be one who is "spiritually poor." Some Jewish expositors believe it refers to corrupt judges.
e. 28:4 The Hebrew word is, "the *Torah*." See also verses 7 and 9.
f. 28:4 As translated from the Aramaic. The Septuagint is, "build a wall to protect themselves."

But those tenderly devoted to the Lord
Can understand justice perfectly.

⁶It's more respectable to be poor and pure
Than rich and perverse.

⁷To be obedient to what you've been taught[a]
Proves you're an honorable child,
But to socialize with the lawless
Brings shame to your parents.

⁸Go ahead and get rich on the backs of the poor,
But all the wealth you gather will one day be given
To those who are kind to the needy.

⁹If you close your heart
And refuse to listen to God's instruction,
Your prayer will be despised.

¹⁰Those who tempt the lovers of God
With an evil scheme
Will fall into their own trap,
But the innocent who resist temptation
Will experience reward.

¹¹The wealthy in their conceit presume to be wise,
But a poor person with discernment
Can see right through them.

¹²The triumphant joy of God's lovers
Releases great glory![b]
But when the wicked rise to power,
Everyone goes into hiding.[c]

¹³If you cover up your sin, you'll never do well;
But if you confess your sins and forsake them,
You will be kissed by mercy.

---

a. 28:7 Or, the *Torah*.
b. 28:12 As translated from the Aramaic.
c. 28:12 Or, "people become victims."

[14]Guard your life carefully and be tender to God
And you will experience His blessings,
But the stubborn, unyielding heart
Will experience even greater evil.

[15]Ruthless rulers can only be compared
To raging lions and roaming bears.[a]

[16]Abusive leaders fail to employ wisdom,
But leaders who despise corruption[b]
Will enjoy a long and full life![c]

[17]A murderer's conscience will torment him—
A fugitive haunted by guilt
All the way to the grave,
With no one to support him!

[18]The pure will be rescued from failure,
But the perverse will suddenly fall into ruin.

[19]Work hard and you'll have all you desire,
But chase a fantasy[d]
And you could end up with nothing.

[20]Life's blessings drench
The honest and faithful person,
But punishment rains down
Upon the greedy and dishonest!

[21]Giving favoritism to the rich and powerful
Is disgusting, and this is the type of judge
Who would betray a man for a bribe.[e]

---

a. 28:15 David, before he killed Goliath, went after the lion and the bear. See 1 Samuel 17:34-37. These beasts represented demonic forces of evil over the land. Daniel also mentions the world's ruthless leaders as lions and bears. See Daniel 7:1-8.
b. 28:16 Or "injustice."
c. 28:16 Or, "enjoy a long reign."
d. 28:19, Or, "an empty dream." The Septuagint is, "the one who pursues leisure."
e. 28:21 As translated from the Aramaic.

²²A greedy manᵃ is in a race to get rich,
But he forgets that he could lose what's
Most important and end up with nothing.ᵇ

²³If you correct someone with constructive criticism,
In the end he will appreciate it more than flattery.

²⁴A person who would rejectᶜ his own parents,
And say, "What's wrong with that?"
Is as bad as a murderer.

²⁵To make rash, hasty decisions
Shows that you are not trusting the Lord,
But when you rely totally on God,
You will still act carefully and prudently.ᵈ
²⁶Self-confidentᵉ know-it-alls
Will prove to be fools;
But when you lean on the wisdom from above,
You will have a way to escape
The troubles of your own making.

²⁷You will never go without if you give to the poor,
But if you're heartless, stingy, and selfishᶠ
You invite curses upon yourself.

²⁸When wicked leaders rise to power,
Good people go into hiding.
But when they fall from power
The godly take their place.

---

a. 28:22 Both the Aramaic and Hebrew have, "The man with an evil eye." This is a figure of speech for a stingy or greedy man. A person who shuts his heart to the poor is said to have an evil eye. A person with a good eye is a person who looks on the poor with generosity.
b. 28:22 As translated from the Aramaic. The Aramaic text sounds so familiar to what Jesus says about gaining the world, but losing our soul. See Mark 8:36.
c. 28:24 As translated from the Septuagint. The Hebrew is, "The one who steals from his own parents."
d. 28:25 As translated from the Septuagint. The Hebrew is, "The greedy person stirs up trouble, but the one who trusts in the Lord will prosper."
e. 28:26 Or, "Those who trust their instincts."
f. 28:27 Or, "He who hides his eyes from the poor."

Chapter 29

Don't Be Stubborn

¹Stubborn people who repeatedly
Refuse to accept correction
Will suddenly be broken
And never recover.

²Everyone rejoices when the lovers of God flourish,
But the people groan
When the wicked rise to power.

³When you love wisdom your father is overjoyed,
But when you associate with prostitutes
You waste your wealth in exchange for disgrace.[a]

⁴A godly leader who values justice
Is a great strength and example to the people.
But the one who sells his influence for money[b]
Tears down what is right.

⁵Flattery can often be used as a trap
To hide ulterior motives
And take advantage of you.

⁶The wicked always have a trap laid for others,
But the lovers of God escape
As they sing and shout in joyous triumph!

⁷God's righteous people will
Pour themselves out for the poor[c]
But the ungodly make no attempt
To understand or help the needy.

You Can't Argue With a Fool

⁸Arrogant cynics love to pick fights
But the humble and wise love to pursue peace.

a. 29:3 See Luke 15:11-24.
b. 29:4 See 1 Timothy 6:10.
c. 29:7 The Hebrew implies standing up for the legal rights of the poor.

⁹There's no use arguing with a fool[a]
For his ranting and raving
Prevents you from making a case
And settling the argument in a calm way.

¹⁰Violent men hate those with integrity,
But the lovers of God
Esteem those who are holy.[b]

¹¹You can recognize a fool by the way
That they give full vent to their anger
And let their words fly!
But the wise bite their tongue
And hold back all they could say.

¹²When leaders listen to false accusations,
Their associates become scoundrels.

¹³Poor people and their oppressors
Have only one thing in common—
God made them both.[c]

¹⁴The best insurance for a leader's longevity
Is to demonstrate justice for the poor.

¹⁵Experiencing many corrections and rebukes
Will make you wise;
But if left to your own ways,
You'll bring disgrace to your parents.[d]

¹⁶When the wicked are in power
Lawlessness abounds,
But the patient lovers of God
Will one day watch in triumph
As their stronghold topples!

---

a. 29:8 The Hebrew implies an argument in a court of law.
b. 29:10 As translated from the Septuagint.
c. 29:13 A figure of speech in Hebrew that can literally be translated, "God gave them both the gift of eyesight." The Septuagint is, "The contracts between lenders and debtors is observed by the Lord."
d. 29:15 As translated from the Septuagint. The Hebrew is, "your mother."

Proverbs 29

¹⁷Correct your child and one day
You'll find he has changed,
And will bring you great delight!

¹⁸When there is no clear prophetic vision[a]
People quickly wander astray.[b]
But when you follow the revelation of the Word[c]
Heaven's bliss fills your soul!

¹⁹A stubborn servant
Can't be corrected by words alone;
For even if he understands,
He pays no attention to you.

²⁰There's only one kind of person
Who is worse than a fool:
The stupid one who speaks
Without thinking first!

²¹If you pamper your servants,
Don't be surprised when they expect
To be treated as sons.[d]

²²The source of strife is found in an angry heart,
For sin surrounds the life of a furious man![e]

²³Lift yourself up with pride
And you will soon be brought low,[f]
But a meek and humble spirit
Will add to your honor.

---

a. 29:18 The Hebrew word used here can refer to "vision of the night," "dream," or "oracle." The Septuagint reads, "Where there is no prophetic seer," or "interpreter."
b. 29:18 Or, "let loose, stripped, or made naked." The Septuagint reads, "the people become lawless."
c. 29:18 Implied in the text. The Hebrew is, *Torah*.
d. 29:21 Or, "If you pamper your servant when he is young, he'll become a weakling in the end." The Septuagint reads, "If you live in luxury as a child, you'll become a domestic (servant), and at last will be grieved with yourself." The Aramaic states, "you'll be uprooted in the end."
e. 29:22 The Hebrew word for *a furious man* is "lord of fury," or "Baal of wrath."
f. 29:23 Or, "to depression."

²⁴You are your own worst enemy
When you partner with a thief,
For a curse of guilt will come upon you
When you fail to report a crime.^a

²⁵Fear and intimidation
Is a trap that holds you back,
But place your confident trust in the Lord
And you will be seated in the high place!

²⁶Everyone curries favor with leaders,
But God is the judge,
And justice comes from Him.

²⁷The wicked hate those who live a godly life,
But the righteous hate injustice
Wherever it's found.

Chapter 30

The Mysterious Sayings of Agur

¹These are the collected sayings
Of the prophet, Agur, Jakeh's son;^b
The amazing revelation^c he imparted
To Ithiel and Ukal.^d

---

a. 29:24 Or, "When under oath to testify, but you do not talk."

b. 30:1 This section of Proverbs is attributed to Agur, who gave these "oracles" to his protégés Ithiel and Ukal. *Agur* means, "to gather a harvest," and was the son of *Jakeh*, which means "blameless" or "obedient." Many Jewish expositors believe that Agur was an imaginary name for Solomon. Nothing further is found about Agur in the Bible than what we have here, which is typical for other prophets mentioned in the Scriptures. Some believe he could be the "master of the collection of sayings" referred to in Ecclesiastes 12:11. *Agur* (taken from Agar) means "collector."

c. 30:1 Or, "mighty prophecy."

d. 30:1 The name *Ithiel* can mean, "God is with me," or, "God has arrived." We know this was fulfilled by Christ, for His birth was the advent, the arrival of God to the earth in human form. *Ukal* means, "I am able," or "I am strong and mighty." When placed together, the meaning of these Hebrew names could read: "Gather a harvest of sons who are blameless and obedient. They will have God with them, and they will be strong and mighty!" This chapter contains some of the most mystical and mysterious sayings found in Proverbs, with hints of revelation from the book of Job.

²God, I'm so weary and worn out,
That I feel more like a beast than a man;
I was made in your image,[a]
But I lack understanding.
³I've yet to learn the wisdom
That comes from the full
And intimate knowledge
Of You, the Holy One.

Six Questions

⁴Who is it that travels back and forth
From the heavenly realm to the earth?[b]
Who controls the wind as it blows[c]
And holds it in His fists?
Who tucks the rain
Into the cloak of His clouds?
Who stretches out the skyline
From one vista to the other?
What is His name?
And what is the name of His Son?
Who can tell me?

A Pure Heart is Filled with God's Word

⁵Every promise from the faithful God
Is pure and proves to be true.
He is a wrap-around shield of protection
For all His lovers
Who run to hide in Him.
⁶Never add to His Words,
Or He will have to rebuke you and
Prove that you're a liar.

⁷God, there are two things I'm asking you for
Before I die,

---

a. 30:2 Implied in the text, which is extraordinarily difficult to translate with certainty.
b. 30:4 Jesus solves this riddle in John 3:13. Only Jesus Christ is the Master of heavenly knowledge and wisdom. See also Ephesians 4:7-10.
c. 30:4 The Hebrew word, *ruach* is also the term used for the Holy Spirit.

Only two:
[8]Empty out of my heart everything that is false,
Every lie, and every crooked thing.
Give me neither undue poverty
Nor undue wealth—
But rather, feed my soul with
The measure of prosperity that pleases You.
[9]May my satisfaction be found in You
And don't let me be so rich
That I don't need You,
Or so poor that I have to resort to
Dishonesty just to make ends meet,
And then my life will never detract
From bringing glory to Your name!

[10]Never defame a servant before his master
For you will be the guilty one
And a curse will come upon you.

[11]There is a generation rising
That curses their fathers
And speaks evil of their mothers!
[12]There is a generation rising
That considers themselves
To be pure in their own eyes[a]—
Yet they are morally filthy,[b]
Unwashed and unclean.
[13]There is a generation rising
That is so filled with pride—
They think they are superior
And look down on others.
[14]There is a generation rising that
Uses their words like swords
To cut and slash those who are different;
And they devour the poor,
The needy, and the afflicted
From off the face of the earth!

a. 30:12 See Judges 21:25.
b. 30:12 The Hebrew uses the word, "excrement."

¹⁵There are three words
To describe the greedy:
"Give me more!"
There are some things that are never satisfied
Forever craving more, they're unable to say,
'That's enough!"
Here are four:
¹⁶The grave, yawning for another victim,
The barren womb, ever wanting a child,
A thirsty soil, ever longing for rain,
And a raging fire, devouring its fuel.
They're all insatiable!

¹⁷The eye that mocks his father
And dishonors his elderly mother^a
Deserves to be plucked out
By the ravens of the valley,
And fed to the young vultures!^b

Four Mysteries

¹⁸There are four marvelous mysteries that are^c
Too amazing to unravel—
Who could fully explain them?^d
¹⁹The way an eagle flies in the sky,^e
The way a snake glides on a boulder,^f

---

a. 30:17 As translated from the Septuagint.
b. 30:17 This is a figure of speech for demonic powers who will remove their vision. Ravens and vultures are unclean birds associated with demonic powers in Hebrew poetry. Typically, the Jewish people are buried in a "valley."
c. 30:18 The Hebrew uses a poetic style of saying there are "three," then saying there are "four mysteries" in order to emphasize their great importance. There could be, within this poetic device, a pointing to the fourth as the key, or the most important.
d. 30:18 Notice that each of these four examples have to do with movement and mystery.
e. 30:19 This is a picture of the overcoming life that soars above our problems and limitations with the wings of an eagle. It could also be a hint of the prophetic revelation that comes to God's servants mysteriously and supernaturally. See Isaiah 40:31 and 1 Corinthians 2:9-13.
f. 30:19 The serpent becomes a picture of our sin that was placed on the Rock, Jesus Christ. How does God remove our sins? It is by the serpent on a Rock. See Numbers 21:6-9; John 3:14-15; and 2 Corinthians 5:21.

The path of a ship as it passes through the sea,[a]
And the way a bridegroom
Falls in love with his bride.[b]

[20]Here is the deceptive way
Of the adulterous woman:[c]
She takes what she wants and then says,
"I've done nothing wrong."

Four Intolerable Things

[21]There are four intolerable events that[d]
Are simply unbearable to observe:
[22]When an unfaithful servant becomes a leader,
When a scoundrel comes into great wealth,
[23]When an unfaithful woman
Marries a good man,
And when a "mistress"
Replaces a faithful wife.

Four Creatures Small and Wise

[24]The earth has four creatures
That are very small but very wise:[e]
[25]The feeble ant has little strength
Yet look how they diligently gather

---

a. 30:19 This is a picture of the way our lives, like a "ship," sail on the high seas of mystery until we reach our destiny. Each of our lives contain mysteries such as, where God decided that we were to be born, how we were raised, the companions that join us, until we reach our desired haven. See Psalm 107:23-30.

b. 30:19 The Hebrew word for "bride" can also be "virgin," pointing to a wedding, thus implying the use of "bridegroom" instead of "man." Consider Ruth and Boaz, but more importantly, this is a beautiful metaphor of the mystery of the love of our heavenly Bridegroom (Jesus) who romances His bride and sweeps us off our feet. See also 2 Corinthians 11:2.

c. 30:20 The adulterous woman of Proverbs is a metaphor of the corrupt religious system. See Revelation 17-18.

d. 30:21 See footnote for 30:18. These four events each depict an undeserved promotion, a displacing of one that is virtuous with one that is corrupt. Each "promotion" indicates that they will carry their corruption with them. The unfaithful servant will likely become a tyrant. The fool who becomes wealthy will squander his wealth. The unfaithful woman (or, 'hated woman') will continue her immorality even married. The girlfriend who replaced the faithful wife will likely find another man one day.

e. 30:24 Or, "they are the epitome of wisdom."

Their food in the summer
To last throughout the winter.[a]
[26]The delicate rock-badger is not all that strong,
Yet look how it makes a secure home,
Nestled in the rocks.[b]
[27]The locusts have no king to lead them
Yet they cooperate as they move forward by bands.[c]
[28]And the small lizard[d] is so easy to catch
As it clings to the walls with his hands,
Yet it can be found inside a king's palace.[e]

Four Stately Things

[29]There are four stately monarchs[f]
Who are impressive to watch as they go forth:
[30]The lion, the king of the jungle, is afraid of no one;
[31]The rooster strutting boldly among the hens[g];
The male goat out in front leading the herd;
And a king leading his regal procession.[h]

[32]If you've acted foolishly
By drawing attention to yourself,
Or if you've thought about
Saying something stupid—
You'd better shut your mouth!

---

a. 30:25 To prepare for the future is a mark of true wisdom.
b. 30:26 This becomes a picture of the believer: though feeling weakness at times, we can make our home in the high place, inside the cleft of the *Rock*. See John 14:1-3.
c. 30:27 The locust army points us to Joel 1 and 2. There is an awakening army coming to devour the works of the enemy. Their King, though invisible, guides them from on high as one army.
d. 30:28 Or "spider."
e. 30:28 Though we may see ourselves as insignificant (like the small lizard), God can place us in very significant places where we can be used for Him.
f. 30:29 See footnote on 30:18.
g. 30:31 As translated from the Septuagint.
h. 30:31 Or, "A king surrounded by his band of soldiers." The Hebrew text is abstruse.

[33]For such stupidity may give you a bloody nose[a]
Because stirring up an argument
Only leads to an angry confrontation!

Chapter 31

King Lemuel's[b] Royal Words of Wisdom

These are the inspired words my mother taught me[c]:

[2]Listen my dear son, son of my womb—
You are the answer to my prayers, my son.
[3]So keep yourself sexually pure
From the promiscuous, wayward woman.
Don't waste the strength of your anointing
On those who ruin kings—
You'll live to regret it![d]
[4]For you are a king, Lemuel,
And it's never fitting for a king
To be drunk on wine
Or for rulers to crave alcohol.
[5]For when they drink they forget justice,
And ignore the rights of those in need,
Those who depend upon you for leadership.[e]
[6-7]Strong drink is given to the terminally ill,
Who are suffering at the brink of death.
Wine is for those in depression

---

a. 30:33 Or, "Churning milk makes butter, punching the nose brings blood, so stirring up anger produces quarrels." The Hebrew contains a word play with the word, "anger," which is almost identical to the word for, "nose."

b. 31:1 Jewish legend is that King Lemuel was a pseudonym for Solomon, which would make his mother, who is mentioned here, Bathsheba. There is no other mention of Lemuel in the Scriptures. Interestingly, "inspired words" is the Hebrew word, *massa*, which some have surmised was a place, meaning, "Lemuel, king of Massa." *Lemuel* means "belonging to God."

c. 31:1 The Septuagint is, "These are the words spoken by God, and through a king came an answer divine."

d. 31:3 As translated from the Septuagint.

e. 31:5 Implied in the text.

In order to drown their sorrows—
Let them drink
And forget their poverty and misery.
[8]But you're to be a king that speaks up
On behalf of the disenfranchised,
And pleads for the legal rights of the
Defenseless and those who are dying.
[9]Be a righteous king, judging on behalf
Of the poor and interceding for
Those most in need.[a]

The Radiant Bride

[10]Who could ever find a wife like this one?[b]
She's a woman of strength and such mighty valor.[c]
She's full of wealth and wisdom,
The price paid for her was greater[d] than many jewels!
[11]Her husband has entrusted his heart to her[e]
For she brings him the rich spoils of victory!
[12]All throughout her life
She brings Him what is good, and not evil.[f]
[13]She searches out continually to possess

---

a. 31:9 See James 1:27.
b. 31:10 Starting with verse 10 thru the end of the book, there is a Hebrew acrostic poem. It is alphabetical in structure with each of the 22 verses beginning with a consecutive Hebrew letter of the alphabet. The implication is that the perfections of this woman will exhaust the entire language. The subject is the perfect bride, the virtuous woman. This woman becomes an incredible picture of the end-time victorious bride of Jesus Christ. She is full of virtue and grace.
c. 31:10 The Hebrew word used to describe this virtuous wife is *chayil*. The meaning of this word cannot be contained by one English equivalent word. It is often used in connection with military prowess. This is a *warring wife*. *Chayil* can be translated, "mighty; wealthy; excellent; morally righteous; full of substance, integrity, abilities, and strength; mighty like an army." The wife is a metaphor for the last day's church, the virtuous, overcoming bride of Jesus Christ. The word *chayil* is most often used to describe valiant men. Because many of the cultural terms and metaphors used in this passage are not understood or even used in today's English speaking world, the translator has chosen to make them explicit.
d. 31:10 Or, "Her worth" The price paid for her was the sacred blood of the Lamb of God, her Bridegroom.
e. 31:11 Or, "has great confidence in her."
f. 31:12 The virtuous bride will not bring disgrace to His name. Jesus will not be ashamed to display her to the world.

That which is pure and righteous.[a]
She delights in the work of her hands.[b]
[14]She gives out revelation-truth[c] to feed others,
Like a trading ship bringing divine supplies[d]
From the merchants.[e]
[15]Even in the night season[f]
She arises[g] and sets food on the table
For hungry ones in her house
And for others.[h]
[16]She sets her heart upon a nation[i]
And takes it as her own, carrying it within her.
She labors there to plant the living vines.[j]

---

a. 31:13 Or, "wool and linen (flax)." Wool is a metaphor often used as a symbol of what is pure. See Isaiah 1:18; Daniel 7:9; and Revelation 1:14. Linen was made from flax and always speaks of righteousness. The priests of the Old Testament wore linen garments as they went before God's presence to offer sacrifice. The curtains of the tabernacle were likewise made of linen, signifying God's righteousness. See Exodus 28:39-43 and Revelation 19:8. The virtuous bride of Christ in the last days will be seeking only what is pure and righteous in the eyes of our Bridegroom.

b. 31:13 Or "eagerly works with her hands." The hands with their five fingers speak of the five ministries of the present work of Christ on the earth: apostles, prophets, evangelists, pastors, and teachers. These are often referred to as the five-fold ministries. Her delight is to equip others and touch those in need.

c. 31:14 Or "bread." This is a consistent emblem of spiritual food.

d. 31:14 Or, "supplies from far away." The implication is from another realm. She is bringing heavenly manna for those she "feeds."

e. 31:14 Or, "like merchant ships bringing goods." Like a ship loaded with cargo, the bride of Christ brings heavenly treasures to others. The use of the term, "merchant" points to Jesus Christ. He is described as a merchant in Matthew 13:45 in the parable of the costly pearl. The "pearl" is the church, or the believer, that cost all that Jesus had (His blood) to purchase us. He is the merchant.

f. 31:15 She is interceding in the night, laboring in a night season to help others.

g. 31:15 The Hebrew word for "arise" can also mean, "to rise up in power." We are told to "Arise and shine for our light has come." See Isaiah 60:1 which uses the same Hebrew word for arise. The bride of Christ will arise with anointing to feed and bless the people of God.

h. 31:15 Or, "female servants." The servants are a metaphor of other churches and ministries.

i. 31:16 Or, "a land, a country."

j. 31:16 Or, "By the fruit of her hands she plants a vineyard." The Septuagint is, "possession." For the hands, see 31:13 footnote. This vineyard becomes a metaphor for the local church. We are the branches of the vine (Christ). See John 15. She is passionate about bringing forth fruit. She becomes a missionary to the nations, planting churches and bringing new life.

[17]She wraps herself in strength,[a]
Might, and power, in all her works.
[18]She tastes and experiences
A better substance,[b]
And her shining light
Will not be extinguished
No matter how dark the night.[c]
[19]She stretches out her hands
To help the needy[d]
And she lays hold of
The wheels of government.[e]
[20]She is known by her extravagant
Generosity to the poor,
For she always reaches out her hands[f]
To those in need.
[21]She is not afraid of tribulation,[g]
For all her household is covered
In the dual garments[h]
Of righteousness and grace!
[22]Her clothing is beautifully knit together[i]—
A purple gown of exquisite linen!
[23]Her husband is famous

---

a. 31:17 Or, "she girds her loins with strength and makes her shoulders strong." This is a figure of speech for being anointed with power to do the works of Jesus. See John 14:12.
b. 31:18 Or, "a good merchandise."
c. 31:18 Her prayer life (lamp) overcomes her circumstances, even in a culture where darkness prevails.
d. 31:19 As translated from the Septuagint. The Hebrew uses a term for "distaff" (a weaver's staff), which is taken from a root word for "prosperity." The poetic nuance of this phrase is that she uses her prosperity to bless the needy.
e. 31:19 Or, "her hands grasp the spindle." This word for "spindle" can also mean, "governmental circuits (wheels)." There is a hint here of the "wheels" mentioned in Ezekiel 1. The throne of God's government sits on flaming wheels. See Daniel 7:9.
f. 31:20 Notice the mention of her "hands." See footnote on 31:13.
g. 31:21 Or, "snow." This is a figure of speech for the fear of a cold winter season.
h. 31:21 As translated from the Septuagint. The Hebrew is, "everyone is covered in scarlet (blood)." Grace has brought righteousness to those in her "house" (under her ministry).
i. 31:22 This garment speaks of the ministries of the body of Christ, woven and knit together by the Holy Spirit. See Ephesians 4:15-16 and Colossians 2:2.

And admired by all,
Sitting as the venerable judge of his people.[a]
[24]Even her works of righteousness[b]
She does[c] for the benefit of her enemies.[d]
[25]Bold power and glorious majesty[e]
Are wrapped around her
As she laughs with joy over the latter days.[f]
[26]Her teachings are filled
With wisdom and kindness,
As loving instruction pours from her lips.[g]
[27]She watches over the ways of her household[h]
And meets every need they have.
[28]Her sons and daughters arise[i] in one accord
To extol her virtues,[j]
And her husband arises to speak of her
In glowing terms.[k]
[29]There are many valiant and noble ones[l]
But you have ascended above them all![m]
[30]Charm can be misleading,

---

a. 31:23 Or, "sitting at the city gates among the elders of the land." Judgment was rendered at the gates of a city in that day. It was their courtroom. Our heavenly King is also the judge. He is so famous, so glorious, yet He is our Bridegroom.
b. 31:24 Or "linen." See footnote for 31:13 regarding linen as a symbol for righteousness.
c. 31:24 Or, "sells them." The root word for "sell" can also mean "surrender."
d. 31:24 Or, "aprons or belts for the Canaanites." The Canaanites were the traditional "enemies" of the Hebrews.
e. 31:25 Or, "beauty, honor, and excellence."
f. 31:25 The virtuous and victorious bride has no fear for the days to come. She contemplates eternity and her forever-union with the Bridegroom.
g. 31:26 The Septuagint is, "She opens her mouth carefully and lawfully."
h. 31:27 Or, "She is a watchman over her house (family)."
i. 31:28 The Hebrew word for "arise" can also mean, "to rise up with power." The Septuagint is, "She raises her children so that they will grow rich."
j. 31:28 Or, "Hooray, hooray for our mother!"
k. 31:28 For more on how the heavenly Bridegroom loves His bride, read the Song of Songs.
l. 31:29 Or, "many daughters have obtained wealth because of her." These valiant and noble ones (daughters) represent the church of previous generations who remained faithful in their pursuit of Jesus. But this final generation will be the bridal company of the lovers of God who do mighty exploits and miracles on the earth.
m. 31:29 Or, "You are first in his eyes." See Song of Songs 6:8-9.

And beauty is vain and so quickly fades,
But this virtuous woman lives in the
Wonder, awe, and fear of the Lord—
She will be praised throughout eternity.[a]
[31]So go ahead and give her the credit that is due her,
For she has become the radiant woman,
And all her loving works of righteousness
Deserve to be admired[b]
At the gateways of every city!

---

a. 31:30 Implied in the context, supplied to complete Hebrew poetic parallelism.
b. 31:31 The Septuagint could be translated, "Her husband is praised at the city gates."

And so ends the Proverbs.
The revelation herein
Will make you a champion.
You will reign in victory
And excel in life.
Wisdom from above
Will pour into your heart
Until you become
An example to your generation.
Live in this book
And wisdom will live in you.

About the Translator

Dr. Brian Simmons is known as a passionate lover of God. After a dramatic conversion to Christ, Brian knew that God was calling him to go to the unreached people of the world and present the gospel of God's grace to all who would listen. He and his wife, Candice, and their three children spent nearly eight years in the tropical rain forest of the Darien Province of Panama as a church planter, translator, and consultant. Brian was involved in the Paya-Kuna New Testament translation project. He studied linguistics and Bible translation principles with New Tribes Mission. After their ministry in the jungle, Brian was instrumental in planting a thriving church in New England (U.S.), and now travels full time as a conference speaker and Bible teacher. He has been happily married to Candice for over forty-two years and is known to boast regularly of his children and grandchildren. Brian and Candice may be contacted at: brian@passiontranslation.com

For more information about the translation project or any of Brian's books please visit:

www.stairwayministries.org

or

www.passiontranslation.com

More from *The Passion Translation*

Luke, to the Lovers of God
Retail Price: $10.95

All four Gospels in our New Testament are inspired by God, but Luke's gospel is unique and distinct. It has been described as the loveliest book ever written. Luke writes clearly of the humanity of Jesus—as the servant of all, and the sacrifice for all. In Luke's gospel, every barrier is broken down between Jew and Gentile, men and women, rich and poor. We see Jesus in Luke as the Savior of all who come to Him.

The Psalms, Poetry on Fire
Retail Price: $19.00

The Psalms, Poetry on Fire translated by Dr. Brian Simmons find the words that express our deepest and strongest emotions. The Psalms will turn your sighing into singing and your trouble into triumph. No matter what you may be going through in your life, the Psalms have a message for you! As you read these 150 poetic masterpieces, your heart will be stirred to worship God in greater ways.

More from *The Passion Translation*

Letters from Heaven by the Apostle Paul
Retail Price: $12.95

Some of the most beautiful and glorious truths of the Bible are found in the letters of the Apostle Paul. Reading through these letters is like having Paul sitting in your living room personally sharing his experience of the power and majesty of God's Word for His people. Be ready to sense the stirring of the Holy Spirit within you as you read *Letters from Heaven by the Apostle Paul.*

Song of Songs (Second Edition)
$9.00

Breathtaking and beautiful, we see the Shulamite's sojourn unveiled in this anointed allegory. It becomes a journey that not only describes the divine parable penned by Solomon, but one that every longing lover of Jesus will find as his or her very own. In *The Passion Translation*™, the translator uses the language of the heart, passionate and loving, to translate the book from Hebrew to English.

"To Establish and Reveal"
For more information visit:
www.5foldmedia.com

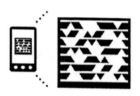

Use your mobile device to scan the tag above and visit our website.
Get the free app:
http://gettag.mobi

Like 5 Fold Media on Facebook, follow us on Twitter!

CPSIA information can be obtained at www.ICGtesting.com
Printed in the USA
LVOW12s0906190813

348488LV00002B/2/P

9 781936 578658